MEMORY AND TRADITION IN ISRAEL

STUDIES IN BIBLICAL THEOLOGY

MEMORY
AND TRADITION
IN ISRAEL

BREVARD S. CHILDS

Yale University Divinity School

ALEC R. ALLENSON, INC.
635 EAST OGDEN AVENUE
NAPERVILLE, ILL.

56432

FIRST PUBLISHED 1962
PRINTED IN GREAT BRITAIN BY
W. & J. MACKAY & CO LTD, CHATHAM

CONTENTS

Preface   6

List of Abbreviations   8

I   LEXICOGRAPHICAL ANALYSIS   9
    A. Occurrence
    B. Etymology
    C. Meaning

II THE HEBREW PSYCHOLOGY OF MEMORY   17

III GOD REMEMBERS   31
    A. Occurrence
    B. Meaning
    C. Form-Critical Analysis

IV ISRAEL REMEMBERS   45
    A. Occurrence
    B. Form-Critical Analysis
    C. Theological Development

V   STUDY OF THE NOUNS   66
    A. *Zikkārôn*
    B. *Zēkher*

VI MEMORY AND CULT   74

VII MEMORY AND HISTORY   81

Index of Authors   91

Index of References   93

PREFACE

WITHIN recent years the important role played by memory in the formulation of Old Testament tradition has been widely recognized. The term has appeared with growing frequency in many popular works which deal with the growth and interpretation of the biblical faith. Still no thorough study has been done on the subject.

The writer began his investigation with the thought of possibly publishing an article. After several months of research it became evident that the material was too vast to include even within a brief monograph. The present study is limited to a discussion of memory within the Old Testament and leaves untouched the rich usage in the post-biblical literature of Rabbinic and Hellenistic Judaism, as well as that of the New Testament.

This monograph focuses on a small area within the Old Testament. It is a study of one Hebrew root as it appears in its nominal and verbal forms. However, from this small point of entry a perspective is won which has widespread implications for understanding the whole of the Old Testament. In a sense, the book is an apology for a return to the detailed work of biblical scholarship. There is here no less concern for the broad theological issues, but a conviction that our grasp of biblical theology grows only as we get past the stage of the general survey.

This study focuses on several main issues. First, we attempt to discover what the Old Testament understands by memory, and what is the scope of its meaning. This entails a detailed discussion of the philological evidence and an investigation of the psychological foundations of memory. Secondly, we strive to discover through a form-critical analysis the context within Israel's life in which memory plays a significant role. This provides a key for interpreting the later theological usage of the term. Thirdly, the theological problem of memory and its relation to tradition is discussed. The familiar problem of the meaning of biblical history is then raised, hopefully with a fresh perspective.

The author is indebted to several men for their aid in writing this monograph. G. Ernest Wright read over the entire manuscript and offered innumerable suggestions for improving both the content and the style. A whole generation of younger American scholars is indebted to his guidance. A deep word of appreciation is due to Professor Gerhard von Rad for his helpful criticisms of the manuscript. He has been of great aid in clarifying the problem. Lastly, the author wishes to express indebtedness to the recent monographs of James Barr, whose incise criticisms of methodology have been a great stimulus.

The SCM Press deserves sincere thanks, not only for its willingness to accept such a technical study, but for the superb quality of its workmanship.

Finally, a word of warm appreciation to my wife, Ann, who has laboured equally hard with me in the writing of this book. Our constant wrestling with the problems of memory, extending over several years, will remain a cherished experience.

New Haven, Conn.   B.S.C.
November 8, 1961

POSTSCRIPT

This study had been completed and submitted to the publisher when the dissertation of Willy Schottroff, *Die Wurzel zkr im Alten Testament* (Mainz, 1961) reached me. This is a superb piece of work both in its philological and exegetical sections. The exhaustive philological study of the root in all the Semitic languages goes far beyond anything which has ever been done, and will certainly be definitive on the subject. In the exegetical section we have often dealt with the same problems and frequently followed a similar discussion of secondary literature. My monograph has concentrated more on the theological problems involved. In our conclusions there are large areas both of agreement and disagreement. While I have greatly profited from Dr Schottroff's work, I feel that there is genuine value in publishing this monograph as an independent piece of research.

New Haven   B.S.C.
December 21, 1961

LIST OF ABBREVIATIONS

ATD	Das Alte Testament Deutsch
BH	*Biblia Hebraica* (3rd ed., 1937), ed. R. Kittel
BK	Biblischer Kommentar
BZ	*Biblische Zeitschrift*
EvTh	*Evangelische Theologie*
EVV	English versions
ExpT	*The Expository Times*
GSAT	*Gesammelte Studien zum Alten Testament*
HUCA	*Hebrew Union College Annual*
IB	*The Interpreter's Bible*
JAOS	*Journal of the American Oriental Society*
JBL	*Journal of Biblical Literature*
LXX	The Septuagint
MT	Masoretic Text
NT	*Novum Testamentum*
ST	*Studia Theologica*
TLZ	*Theologische Literaturzeitung*
TZ	*Theologische Zeitschrift*
VT	*Vetus Testamentum*
ZAW	*Zeitschrift für die alttestamentliche Wissenschaft*
ZDPV	*Zeitschrift des Deutschen Palästinavereins*
ZTK	*Zeitschrift für Theologie und Kirche*

I

LEXICOGRAPHICAL ANALYSIS

A. OCCURRENCE

THE verb *zākhar* (to remember) occurs in the Old Testament 169 times in the qal form, 19 times in the niphal, and 41 times in the hiphil.[1] The noun *zikkārôn* (memorial sign) appears 22 times in its singular form, twice in the plural, and once in its Aramaic cognate. The noun *zēkher* (name) appears 23 times. Two other nouns occur infrequently, *'azkārāh*[2] (memorial offering), and the Aramaic *dokhrân* (record), but these are peripheral for our study. Finally, several proper names are formed from the root, *zakkûr* (Zaccur), *zikhrî* (Zichri), *zēkher* (Zecher), and *zĕkharyāh*, *zĕkharyāhû* (Zechariah).

B. ETYMOLOGY

The etymology of the Hebrew root *zkr* is unknown. The root is cognate with a common Semitic root appearing in Akkadian, Arabic, Ethiopic, Aramic, and occurs in a Canaanite gloss of the Amarna letters. In the history of Hebrew lexicography several notable attempts have been made to solve the etymological problem, particularly during the latter part of the last century.[3]

---

[1]The terms 'qal', 'niphal', and 'hiphil' will be used throughout this monograph. It is important for the reader who lacks a knowledge of Hebrew to understand these distinctions of grammar. The Hebrew language achieves different aspects of the primary meaning of the verb by means of a system of 'conjugations', often called 'stems'. The root meaning of the verb is the qal; the passive or reflexive is the niphal; the causative is the hiphil.

[2]This noun occurs seven times and is confined to the Priestly source. It is that portion of the meal offering which is burnt. Its etymology and meaning remain unclear. Cf. L. Koehler, *Lexicon in Veteris Testamenti Libros* (Leiden, 1953) *s.v.* for a list of suggested etymologies.

[3]The Arabic *dâl* and the Aramaic *dāleth* point to an initial interdental consonant in the proto-Semitic form. Most frequently the attempt has been made to connect the root *zkr* (to remember) with the noun *zākhār* (male), which also evidences the interdental. Gesenius, in the first edition of his

There has emerged no consensus and recent lexicographers usually prefer to leave the problem unsolved.

C. MEANING

(1) Qal

It is no easy task to determine the range of meaning attached to this verb. We begin with the qal. The lexicon of Brown, Driver and Briggs,[1] after dividing the material into two categories according to whether it has a human or divine subject, classifies the verb according to its object. The resulting distinctions show little more than shades of variation on the basic meaning of 'remember'. One 'remembers', 'calls to mind', 'recalls' past events, conditions, and persons which he has once experienced (Deut. 7.18; Job 11.16; Esth. 2.1). There is a slight shift of meaning when the emphasis turns from the recalling of the past to a preoccupation with the present and the future. The word comes to mean 'keep in mind', 'be attentive to', or 'consider' (Deut. 8.18; Isa. 47.7; Jer. 51.50). When used in reference to persons, a resultant quality of action is included: 'remember for good or evil' (Gen. 40.14; Neh. 6.14). Finally, Brown, Driver and Briggs distinguish a meaning of remember as 'commemorate' (Ex. 13.3).

Thesaurus, accepted an earlier interpretation that *zākhār* as the male was conceived of as the sex through which the memory of parents and ancestors was propagated. In the later editions of his lexicon he proposed another interpretation which then became widespread. The origin of the root lay in the idea of pricking or piercing, whence came the noun as the *membrum virile.* The idea of memory came from that of penetrating or fixing in the mind (cf. *A Hebrew and English Lexicon,* translated by E. Robinson, 20th ed., Boston, 1886). Gesenius's theory was attacked by F. Schwally, *ZAW* 11 (1891), pp. 176 ff., who noted the lack of evidence that the Semitic root ever carried the meaning proposed. He suggested that the noun *zēkher* designated originally the invoking of the name of the deity in the cult and that *zākhār* is the cultic person. This hypothesis was contested from two different sides. B. Jacob, *ZAW* 17 (1897), pp. 71 ff., denied that the cultic meaning of *zēkher* was original. Also I. Peritz, *JBL* 17 (1898), p. 112, felt that Schwally's reconstruction was unlikely since it defended an etymological development which moved from an initially spiritualized meaning to a later physical sense. Most recently, M. Seidel, *Lĕshônēnû* 20 (1956), pp. 45–6, has attempted to establish a common root for *zkr* and *zkh* with the basic meaning of pierce. However, this hardly recommends itself.

[1] *A Hebrew and English Lexicon of the Old Testament* (Oxford, 1907).

Similarly, the lexicon of Gesenius-Buhl recognizes in the qal only different nuances of the basic meaning: 'to recall something, which is already known, to keep in mind'.[1] L. Koehler's classification is determined largely by the various ways in which the verb is syntactically linked to its object, but again he finds only slight variation.[2]

In spite of this general agreement among lexicographers, there remains a central problem. Has the essential character of the verb as an expression of Hebrew mentality been adequately described? What are we to understand by the term 'remember'? How does the Old Testament conceive of thought as related to event? J. Pedersen raises a basic issue with his accustomed acumen when he suggests that the verb expresses a uniquely Hebrew category.[3] In the next chapter we shall attempt to test his thesis, since the scope of the question extends far beyond the boundaries controlled by lexicography.

(2) Hiphil

The problem of determining the basic meaning of the hiphil is more complex and controversial. This difficulty reflects itself in the wide range of meanings and the conflicting categories under which the verb is treated. The question has been most recently reviewed by Begrich,[4] Stamm,[5] and Reventlow.[6]

In our opinion, the key to an understanding of the hiphil lies in distinguishing between two clear and distinct circles of meaning, the one cultic, the other juridical. Because of a general failure to distinguish between these meanings, attempts have often been made to force all the material into an artificial category.

(a) The Cultic

The hiphil occurs in a set formula with the noun *šēm* (name).

[1] *Hebräisches und Aramäisches Handwörterbuch über das Alte Testament* (17 Aufl., Leipzig, 1921). Gesenius-Buhl does recognize the qal meaning 'erwähnt werden' (mention) which has been recently re-emphasized by N. Berggrün, '*zkr = hizkîr* = utter' (Hebrew), *Lĕshônēnû* 21 (1957), pp. 279–82, and J. Blau, *VT* 11 (1961), pp. 81–6.

[2] L. Koehler, *op. cit.*

[3] J. Pedersen, *Israel*, I–II (London, Copenhagen, 1926), p. 106.

[4] J. Begrich, 'Sōfēr und Mazkîr', *ZAW* 58 (1940/41), pp. 12 f.

[5] J. J. Stamm, 'Zum Altargesetz im Bundesbuch', *TZ* 1 (1945), pp. 304 ff.

[6] H. Graf Reventlow, 'Das Amt des Mazkir', *TZ* 15 (1959), pp. 161–75.

The verb occurs six times with this noun as direct object (Ex. 20. 24; 23.13; II Sam. 18.18; Isa. 26.13; 49.1; Ps. 45.18), four times with the preposition *bĕ* (Josh. 23.7; Amos 6.10; Isa. 48.1; Ps. 20.8), and once with the conjunction *kî*. The suggestion was first advanced by Jacob[1] and again independently by Begrich[2] that the hiphil be interpreted as a denominative of *zēkher*, 'to name the name'. While this remains a hypothesis, it seems to offer the most satisfactory explanation.[3] The hiphil in Hebrew would then be equivalent in meaning to the basic stem in Akkadian, *zakâru*.

The two earliest occurrences of the hiphil appear in the Book of the Covenant. Commentators are divided on how to interpret Ex. 23.13: 'the name of other gods you shall not *tazkîrû* nor let such be heard out of your mouth.' Driver[4] thinks that the contrast is between not even mentioning their names, still less invoking them in worship. This interpretation has not taken seriously enough the obvious cultic background of *hizkîr šēm*. To name the name of other gods is the basic form of Semitic worship. Grether reconstructs the background of the naming of the deity in other Semitic religions and comments: '. . . one can conclude that the name stood in a particularly close relationship with the cult. Indeed, the pronouncement of the name was considered one of the most important moments of the cult.'[5] We feel that the denominative usage would fit well in this passage.

The interpretation of the other early passage is even more controversial. Ex. 20.24 reads: 'In every place where *'azkîr 'eth-šĕmî* (I cause my name to be remembered) I will come to you and bless

---

[1] B. Jacob, 'Beiträge zu einer Einleitung in den Psalmen', *ZAW* 17 (1897), pp. 69 ff.

[2] Begrich, *op. cit.*, p. 12.

[3] Cf. H. Bauer, P. Leander, *Historische Grammatik der hebräischen Sprache des Alten Testaments* (Halle, 1922), p. 293, for the use of the hiphil in a denominative sense. J. Blau, *op. cit.*, has recently taken up an older suggestion of J. Barth that *zkr* had originally an i-imperfect *yazkir*, with the meaning 'mention'. The hiphil later displaced the qal i-imperfect and was assigned its original meaning. We do not feel that this explanation is correct. The meaning of 'mention' does not seem primary to the qal (cf. Berggrün, *op. cit.*). Jacob's suggestion (*op. cit.*) to take the hiphil as a denominative seems far more likely.

[4] S. R. Driver, *The Book of Exodus* (Cambridge, 1911), p. 241.

[5] O. Grether, *Name und Wort Gottes im Alten Testament* (Giessen, 1934), p. 19.

you.' J. J. Stamm has suggested that the sentence should be translated: 'at every place in which I reveal my name . . .'[1] He cites as parallels Isa. 26.13; Isa. 12.4; and Ps. 45.18, where *hizkîr šēm* means 'to proclaim the name (of God)'. Although this interpretation is cited by Koehler,[2] apparently it has not been accepted; rather, he gives to this passage the meaning 'cause to be remembered' and cites II Sam. 18.18 as its parallel. According to Koehler's interpretation, which is the traditional one, the verse refers to Yahweh's causing his name to be remembered in Israel only at designated places. The issue, then, is whether the meaning is: *a.* Yahweh reveals his name at chosen places, or *b.* Yahweh establishes a cult to remember his name at chosen places.

II Sam. 18.18 has been cited as a parallel. Absolom set up a pillar because he had no son *baʿăbhûr hazkîr šěmî*. Usually this phrase is translated 'to cause my name to be remembered'. But this assumes rather than proves that *hizkîr šēm* carries the meaning of 'cause to remember'. A translation which is more consistent with the above examples would be: 'I have no son to pronounce my name.' The connection of the stele with the naming of the dead suggests some sort of cultic practice performed for the dead.[3]

In the light of the close parallel in Ex. 23.13 where the meaning is clear, we are strongly inclined to accept Stamm's interpretation. Ex. 20.24 is significant in showing the ancient tendency within Yahwism to check the magical usage of the name within the cult. Stamm is not convinced that the hiphil must be taken as a denominative. Nevertheless, this verse would lend itself admirably to such an interpretation.

We turn now to four passages in which *běšēm* occurs (Josh.

---

[1] Stamm, *op. cit.*, p. 305.

[2] L. Koehler, *loc. cit.*

[3] There is an interesting parallel in the Old Aramaic inscription Panammu I (*Hadadinschrift*). (Cf. M. Lidzbarski, *Handbuch der nordsemitischen Epigraphik*, I [Weimar, 1898], pp. 440 ff.; G. A. Cooke, *A Text-Book of North-Semitic Inscriptions* [Oxford, 1903], pp. 159 ff.) Panammu erects a statue to Hadad and enjoins his son after his death to sacrifice to Hadad and to 'remember the name of Hadad' (line 16: *wyzkr ʾšm hdd*). Moreover, the son must also 'remember the name of Panammu' (line 21: *wyzkr ʾšm pnmw*) and say: 'May the soul of Panammu eat with Hadad', etc. Cf. the interesting material in K. Galling, 'Erwägungen zum Stelenheiligtum von Hazor', *ZDPV* 75 (1959), pp. 1–13, and W. F. Albright, *Suppl. to VT*, 4 (1957), p. 251.

23.7; Amos 6.10; Isa. 48.1; Ps. 20.8).[1] Here a slight shift in meaning is discernible. Instead of the direct object the idiom has become 'to invoke with the name of' God. In two cases it stands parallel to the verb 'swear by' (*niśbaʿ*). The background of this expression is clear. It is a technical cult expression similar to the more frequent expression 'to call upon the name of Yahweh' (*qārāʾ běšēm yhwh*), possibly with originally magical overtones.[2]

Especially in the later Hebrew the verb undergoes a decided broadening. Isa. 12.4 still uses the hiphil in conjunction with the name, but now with the meaning of 'praise' or 'confess' and parallel to 'give thanks' (*hôdhāh*). The object of the verb, used in this broader sense of 'praise', now includes the deeds of Yahweh (Ps. 77.12), his righteousness (Ps. 71.16), his steadfast love (Isa. 63.7), etc. Most probably it occurs with this same meaning, although without an object, in two superscriptions (Ps. 38.1; 70.1).

There is one instance (Isa. 66.3) of a late cultic usage in which the verb is an obvious denominative of the noun *ʾazkārāh* (memorial offering) and means 'to make a memorial offering'.

(*b*) The Juridical

It has been often observed that the hiphil occurs within a technical forensic setting. There are six examples of the formula 'to cause to remember sin' (*hizkîr ʿāwôn*—Num. 5.15; I Kings 17.18; Ezek. 21.28, 29 [EVV: 23, 24]; 29.16; *hizkîr hēṭʾ*—Gen. 41.9). The sense of the expression in these passages is clearly that of accusing or making sin known. In Num. 5.15 the purpose of the ordeal of the suspected wife is to make sin known, not to remind the wife nor others to whom the sin is unknown. Likewise, the widow fears that Elijah has come to accuse her of sin (I Kings 17.18).

J. Begrich[3] was the first to point out the forensic background of Isa. 43.26:

'*hazkîrēnî*, let us argue together
Set forth your case, that you may be proved right.'

---

[1]The LXX suggests a different reading in Ps. 20.8 (cf. *BH*). In Isa. 48.1 *běšēm* appears in close parallelism with *hizkîr*, and is, therefore, included.

[2]Grether, *op. cit.*, p. 19. Cf. also M. Greenberg, 'The Hebrew Oath Particle Ḥay/Ḥē', *JBL* 76 (1957), pp. 34–9.

[3]J. Begrich, *Studien zu Deuterojesaja* (Stuttgart, 1938), p. 26, and again *ZAW* 58 (1940/41), p. 12.

The usual translation 'put me in remembrance' completely misses the parallelism. The form is the appellation of the accused who demands a trial. The verb should be translated with some such phrase as 'accuse me'.

The office of the *mazkîr* (recorder) has long been a puzzle. It appears in the list of functionaries serving under David and Solomon (II Sam. 8.16; II Sam. 20.24; I Kings 4.3; I Chron. 18.15). Begrich[1] identified the position with that of a high court office found in Egypt which David had appropriated. Recently, Reventlow[2] has proposed a revision of this thesis. He sees the office of the *mazkîr* as rooted in the ancient tribal amphictyony. He is the official prosecutor (the Director of Public Prosecutions or Attorney-General in modern terminology) whose duty it is to prosecute all breaches of law. He is the 'accuser' *par excellence*. This interpretation is able to explain well such passages as Ezek. 21.28 (EVV: 24). In a symbolic act the prophet designates the king of Babylon as *mazkîr* to accuse Israel of her sin. Likewise, Isa. 62.6 seems to be a prophetic application of this basic idea.[3]

This forensic sense of *hizkîr* also underwent a broadening. The verb occurs with the more general meaning of 'to make known' or 'to mention' (Gen. 40.14; I Sam. 4.18; Isa. 19.17; Jer. 4.16; Ps. 87.4).

To summarize: It is apparent that the juridical meaning of the hiphil is not a denominative and thus differs from the cultic. However, the two usages share the common sense of *hizkîr* as the act of utterance rather than the act of remembering. The name is spoken or the accusation is pronounced.

---

[1] J. Begrich, 'Sōfēr und Mazkīr', *ZAW* 58 (1940/41).

[2] H. Graf Reventlow, *op. cit.*, pp. 161–75.

[3] H. J. Boecker, 'Erwägungen zum Amt des Mazkir', *TZ* 17 (1961), pp. 212 ff., objects to Reventlow's proposal on several grounds. He feels that the double function of prosecutor and defender, which he claims for the verb, cannot be united in one office. Secondly, he contests Reventlow's interpretation of the niphal usages in Ezekiel as offering evidence of an office of prosecutor. Boecker suggests that the *mazkîr* is an activity (*Tätigkeit*) within the trial, open to every citizen, in which testimony is given either for or against the defendant. This function he distinguishes from the 'royal recorder'. We feel that the issue has not been finally settled. In our opinion, a more careful distinguishing between the stem forms of *zkr* would help. Cf. our criticism of Reventlow below, p. 33.

(3) Niphal

The relation of the niphal to the qal and hiphil is not always easy to determine with certainty. Frequently the niphal occurs as a passive of the qal and is used in a sense which is closely akin to the root meaning of the qal (Isa. 65.17). In four cases it is used idiomatically in the sense of not to be remembered is not to exist (Isa. 23.16; 65.17; Ezek. 21.37 [EVV: 32]; 25.10). The niphal as a passive of qal carries the meaning to be commemorated (Esth. 9.28) and to be mentioned (Job 28.18).

However, there are cases in which the niphal is to be clearly understood as a passive of the hiphil. At times the cultic sense of the hiphil is reflected in the niphal. There are four examples in which the verb is joined to the noun *šēm* (name) (Hos. 2.19 [EVV: 17]; Jer. 11.19; Zech. 13.2; Ps. 83.5). The fact that there is only one instance of the qal connected with this noun (Ps. 119.55) would confirm its relation to the hiphil. In these cases the denominative usage seems appropriate.

There are other examples in which the forensic element dominates. In spite of the fact that the qal can carry juridical meaning, the stereotyped phraseology within the oracles of Ezekiel points to the niphal as the passive of the juridical class of hiphil (Ezek. 3.20; 18.22, 24; 33.13, 16). Reventlow suggests that the priest has assumed the role of the representative of Yahweh and pronounces a judgment within the cult.[1]

Summary: The lexicographical analysis is significant in revealing the complexity of the root *zkr* and the danger of confusing fundamentally divergent meanings. Two basic meanings can be distinguished: *a.* to remember, in the qal, *b.* to utter, in the hiphil. The latter can either be a cultic naming of the name or a juridical accusation of sin. It is important that these distinctions be observed in any attempt to understand the meaning of memory in the Old Testament. The qal must be investigated independently of the hiphil and the proposed connection established rather than assumed.[2]

[1] Reventlow, *op. cit.,* pp. 172–4.
[2] H. M. Sykes, 'The Eucharist as "Anamnesis"', *ExpT* 71 (1960), pp. 115 ff., uses as a starting-point for a study of memory in the Old Testament the close connection of *zkr* with the name. Because this connection is found only in the hiphil, the conclusions drawn can be questioned.

II

THE HEBREW PSYCHOLOGY OF MEMORY

OLD Testament scholars have been slow in recognizing the peculiar features of memory within the Old Testament. One searches in vain for a significant treatment of the subject among older writers. It was not until the appearance of the stimulating book of J. Pedersen, *Israel* (1926), that the problem was forcefully raised. Pedersen not only recognized a problem, but he offered a comprehensive theory to explain the unusual features.

Pedersen suggested that the Israelitic approach to life could be classified as 'primitive'.[1] The Hebrew viewed reality with the purpose of discovering a totality. This concern reflected itself in the psychological terms employed. Man, in his total essence, is a *nepheš* (soul). The will or volition is not an independent feature, but 'the tendency of the totality of the soul'. The term *lēbb* (heart) designates the self when it functions as operative power. As a result the relationship between thought and action differs radically from that conceived of by the modern. Theoretical, objective thinking which is divorced from the will is unknown. The Hebrew understands as thought the process by which an image enters the heart and immediately influences the will. Thought which does not lead to action is a meaningless flash.

Then Pedersen turned his attention to the verb 'remember' which is frequently used in parallelism with verbs 'to think'. His classic formulation is as follows: 'When the soul remembers something, it does not mean that it has an objective memory image of some thing or event, but that this image is called forth in the soul and assists in determining its direction, its action. . . . The peculiarity about the Israelite is that he cannot at all imagine memory, unless at the same time an effect on the totality and its direction of will is taken for granted.'[2]

[1] J. Pedersen, *Israel*, I–II, pp. 99 ff.   [2] *Ibid.*, pp. 106–7.

It is our concern to examine Pedersen's theory of memory and to see if his suggestion can be sustained that special categories are operative in which thought and action are considered part of a totality. A re-examination of the material is particularly in order because of the recent full-scale attack on Pedersen's method by James Barr.[1]

We shall begin by reviewing the evidence deduced by Pedersen in defence of his theory of memory. Because many of Pedersen's ideas are only briefly suggested rather than elaborated, we shall take the liberty of developing his implicit ideas on the basis of his own method.

(1) In the first place, the verb *zkr* appears frequently in direct parallelism with verbs denoting an action: to bless (Ps. 115.12), to set free (Ps. 136.23), to show favour (Ps. 106.4), to punish (Jer. 14.10). In passages in which there is no direct parallelism, nevertheless, the act of remembering seems closely linked with action of some kind (cf. I Sam. 1.19 f.; Judg. 16.28, etc.).

(2) Synonyms which a modern reader might classify as expressing merely a mental process are often regarded in the Old Testament as effecting an external event. (For *hgh* [mutter] which is parallel to *zkr* in Ps. 63.7, cf. Ps. 115.7; for *syh* [consider] which is parallel to *zkr* in Ps. 77.13, cf. Ps. 69.13; for *hsb* [think] which is parallel to *zkr* in Ps. 77.7, cf. Jer. 23.27.)

(3) The most frequently used antonym is the verb *skh* (forget) which appears over ten times in connection with *zkr*. Forgetting is not a psychological act of having a thought pass from one's consciousness, but an outward act of worshipping other gods (Deut. 8.19), of forsaking someone (Isa. 49.14), of not keeping the commandments (Deut. 8.11). However, the frequent identification of the verb with an action does not eliminate the process of thought which is involved in the act. Because the thought inevitably leads to the act, the two are often fused. The recognition of the thought as an entity in itself appears clearly in those cases in which a time interval separates the thought from its fulfilment in the act (Jer. 44.21).

(4) The most important idiom for revealing the psychology of memory is formed with verbs which are connected with the heart.

[1] *The Semantics of Biblical Language* (Oxford, 1961).

Three verbs appear in this idiom in parallelism with *zkr*: *śym* (to set—II Sam. 19.20; Isa. 57.11; Isa. 47.7); *'lh* (to lift up—Jer. 3.16; 44.21; 51.50); *hēšîbh* (to restore—Isa. 46.8).

We shall turn our attention to the idiom with *śym*. The most frequent phrase is 'to set the thing upon his heart' (*śām 'ēth haddābhār 'al libbô*). There are other syntactical possibilities by which the verb governs its object,[1] but with little shift in meaning. More significant are the two forms of the idiom. One can set his heart to a thing or set a thing to one's heart. These two expressions are used interchangeably and, according to Pedersen, reflect the same approach to the psychology of thought. When one sets his heart to a thing, it means that the whole self is directed to it. The heart is the self in action. One cannot relate himself to a thing except through the heart, which means that the will must be involved. Because the Egyptians did not set their hearts to the words of Yahweh, their cattle were left to destruction in the fields (Ex. 9.21). The Egyptians did not relate themselves to the words of Yahweh in terms of the will which meant that no action was involved. Again, Shimei does not want the king to set his heart to his treason, because this will lead to a sentence of death (II Sam. 19.20). Or, David took to heart a word that all his sons had been killed. Even though the word was false, a commensurate action followed. He rent his garments, etc. (II Sam. 13.33). The idiom has a similar meaning when used with the other two verbs *'lh* and *hēšîbh*.

According to Pedersen this idiom clarifies the Hebrew understanding of the process of thought.[2] A thought arises and enters upon the heart. The heart as the operative power immediately effects the action. Because these component parts are seen as one totality, thought upon the heart is often viewed as an event, since this leads inevitably to the action. The characteristic feature of Hebrew mentality is in refusing to see thought as an objective image to which volition must be added to produce an action. An image must be joined to will even to be regarded as thought.

We turn now to James Barr's criticism of Pedersen's method. His criticism can be summarized under three headings:

[1] The prepositions *'el*, *lĕ*, and *bĕ* also occur.
[2] Pedersen, *op. cit.*, pp. 107 f.

(1) Pedersen attempts to see in the structure of the Hebrew language a reflection of a Hebrew mentality. He does this either by working with various lexical terms which, he assumes, reflect in their distance different aspects of the thought structure, or by seeking directly to relate a syntactical construction to a mental pattern. According to Barr such an attempted correspondence faces grave difficulties. It fails to recognize the arbitrary character of words which is a fundamental law of synchronistic linguistics. Moreover, it fails to recognize the complexity of establishing a simple connection because of the historical factor.[1]

(2) Pedersen fails to examine the Hebrew language as a whole, and treats it in isolation from other relevant linguistic material.[2]

(3) Pedersen tries to reconstruct from the Old Testament certain unique categories which he calls 'primitive' on the basis of a theory of prelogical mentality. However, these categories do not arise from the material itself, but are imposed upon it.[3]

We shall restrict the discussion of the above criticisms to their effect on the problem of memory and seek to determine to what degree Barr's criticisms of Pedersen are justified.

Linguistic Structure and Mental Pattern

Pedersen seeks to determine the meanings carried by the verb *zkr* by examining the different contexts in which the word appears. This entails a study of paralleled expressions, synonyms and antonyms. Barr would have no criticism up to this point. However, Pedersen goes one step farther. He suggests that, because the verb can mean both to think and to act, these two processes are not distinguished in Hebrew mentality. In other words, a lexical overlapping reflects a similar state within the thought structure. Barr terms this an 'illegitimate identity transfer'. He offers many examples to show that it is a common linguistic phenomenon for a verb to carry several meanings, and that this does not imply a semantic identification.

In our opinion, Barr has touched upon a fundamental weakness in Pedersen's theory. Pedersen has noticed that the word *zkr* is used in various contexts, frequently with a sense which includes

[1]Barr, *op. cit.*, pp. 30 ff., 34 ff.   [2]*Ibid.*, p. 25.
[3]*Ibid.*, pp. 30 ff.

far more than subjective recalling. 'To remember' often bears a meaning which we would describe as characterizing an action. However, this discovery only reveals that the Hebrew use of the word 'remember' is more inclusive than that of English. The verb has a wider semantic range. Barr is correct in insisting that no conclusions can be drawn from this use of words regarding different mentalities.

However, one is not doing justice to Pedersen's method in supposing that he is simply trying to establish a correlation between linguistic structure and mental pattern. The issue is much more complex than this. Pedersen's book presupposes the traditio-historical method used throughout the latter part of the nineteenth and early twentieth centuries, which attempted to recover the institutions forming Israel's patterns of oral tradition. Pedersen set as his task to understand Israel's mentality by reconstructing some of her basic institutions such as family, war, cult and kingship. Yet he soon discovered that many of Israel's institutions revealed signs of 'primitive' or mythopoeic roots. He felt, for example, that a totality concept of the soul was basic to Israel's thought structure. However, he encountered a fundamental difficulty. The sources are such as to prevent an easy recovery and the original patterns appear only in broken form. He, therefore, attempted his own reconstruction of Ancient Israel's thought structure into which he fitted the fragments.

Basically, the approach of Pedersen did not seek to discover a picture of Israel's mentality directly from the syntax, or to establish a 'vocabulary stock', as Barr tends to imply. Rather, he found signs in the use of words which pointed to vestiges of a mythopoeic view of the world. From the vantage-point of the larger perspective he then sought to reconstruct Israel's thought world. For example, the fact that *dābhār* can denote both word and event does not necessarily imply a reflection of a mental pattern in which these are identified. However, when the mythopoeic background of *dābhār* within the cult is uncovered, it becomes apparent that the primitive mind conceived of these two entities as one.[1] Pedersen's theory of memory is an attempt to show that the word

[1]Barr's treatment of *dābhār, op. cit.,* pp. 127 ff., in our opinion, fails to come to grips seriously with this dimension of the problem.

zkr belongs within a similar mythopoeic framework as he had discovered for *dābhār*. Memory and event were not separated, but seen as part of one totality.

While we agree in principle with Pedersen's method, the decisive question is whether or not Pedersen can demonstrate in a specific synchronistic context that *zkr* still carries mythopoeic connotations. In our opinion, his evidence for *zkr* has not been conclusive. The verb denotes both a process of thought and an action, but there is no real evidence which demands a semantic identification. Pedersen's evidence for the verb only shows a wider semantic range to be present in Hebrew, but not mythopoeic thought patterns.

The same issue is involved in Pedersen's argument on the basis of the idiom 'to set the thing upon his heart'. Again Pedersen's method is not to be misconstrued as being a naïve reading of a mental pattern from an idiomatic expression. He was obviously aware of the stereotyped quality of an idiom and that such a phrase as 'his heart went out to the suffering child' offers no insight into modern man's approach to reality. Rather, he sought to show the mythopoeic roots of such basic terms as soul, heart, and spirit in order to recover a total picture of the psychological world of Ancient Israel in which thought and action seemed closely allied.

It would appear that Pedersen was on more solid ground here, since there are many usages of the term 'heart' which clearly reveal an original mythopoeic frame of reference common to primitive cultures. The heart can be strengthened by food (Gen. 18.5), and become fat (Isa. 6.10). Largeness of heart implies physical well-being (I Kings 5.9). Conversely, one can lose the heart (Prov. 6.32 f.). It can melt away (Josh. 7.5), or wither (Ps. 102.5). The mythopoeic element lies in the causality principle which connects the physical and volitional aspects of the heart.

While it is true that the use of the term 'heart' arose out of a mythopoeic background, and often requires a 'realistic'[1] and not figurative interpretation, yet there are other examples in which this usage has been completely lost. Barr is certainly right in insisting that each usage must be determined from its specific

---

[1] For a discussion of this terminology, cf. C. Barth, *Die Errettung vom Tode* (Zürich, 1947), pp. 16 ff.

context. Now, in the examples cited in which the idiom with the heart appears in parallelism with *zkr*, there seems to be no compelling evidence to show that a mythopoeic flavour is still present. In Ex. 9.21 the idiom simply means that the Egyptians 'did not pay attention to' the words of Yahweh. More cannot be inferred from the expression. Again, Shimei does not want the king 'to bear in mind' his treason (II Sam. 19.20).

We conclude, therefore, that Pedersen has not, in fact, been able to show that a different mental relationship exists between memory and action which sets the Old Testament apart from the modern. He has shown only that the verb *zkr* has a wider semantic range in which thought and action are both included.

The Problem of Isolation

Barr's second criticism deals with Pedersen's treatment of the Hebrew language in isolation from other relevant linguistic material. Certainly Pedersen would not defend in principle a method of isolation and would have answered in his own defence that the selecting of any area of research necessitates setting limits. He conceived his task to be the investigating of the thought patterns of Israel alone, which is certainly a legitimate task. However, the danger of *unconsciously* making value-judgments regarding the uniqueness of Israel's thought is present, even if one recall that Pedersen has been careful not to make wide generalizations contrasting Greek and Hebrew mentality which is characteristic of the work of Boman.[1]

In the light of Barr's criticism we should like to set Pedersen's evidence regarding memory in the Old Testament within a broader framework and seek to make some comparisons.

The verb *zkr* appears frequently in North-west Semitic inscriptions. The earliest occurrence appears in a Canaanite gloss to the Amarna texts (228.19):[2] 'May the king, my Lord, remember (*ia-az-ku-ur-mi*) everything which has been done against Hazur,

[1] T. Boman, *Hebrew Thought compared with Greek* (ET, London, 1960).
[2] J. A. Knudtzon, *Die El-Amarna-Tafeln* (Leipzig, 1909), p. 768. *The Assyrian Dictionary*, vol. 21 (Chicago, 1961), p. 22, lists two other occurrences of *zakâru* in the Amarna texts with a similar meaning of 'remember' (147.23; 289.41), and notes that the word with this meaning was borrowed from the West Semitic.

your city, and against your servant.' This use of *zkr* is similar to that found frequently in the Old Testament and signifies the recalling of a past event which issues in favourable action toward its recipient. Similarly, in the Lachish Letters (II.4)[1] Hoshaiah addresses Ya'osh with a typical stereotyped formula: 'Who is your servant but a dog that my lord has remembered (*zkr*) his servant.' Remember is again not in the sense of merely to recall in thought, but to act toward (cf. I Sam. 25.31).

Frequently, the deity is the subject of the desired response. In a Phoenician votive inscription inscribed on a statue of Melqarth (Larnax Lapēthos 2.15)[2] Yathanba'al requests the deity in response to his sacrifice: 'May Melqarth remember me (*yskrn*).' Similarly, Nabataean and Palmyrene inscriptions, as well as those from Hatra, and countless examples of Jewish sepulchural inscriptions record the stereotyped expressions 'that NN may be remembered for good' (*dkyr lṭb*) before the deity, or that 'NN may be remembered in mercy and peace' (*dkyr bṭb wšlm*).[3]

The Old Aramaic inscription of Panammu I (*Hadadinschrift*) from the eighth century BC preserves the pěʿal form of *zkr* in a blessing and curse formula: '(whoever) shall moreover remember (*yzkr*) the soul of Panammu with Hadad . . .' (line 17).[4] To remember in this context describes a cultic act in which a rite is performed to incur favour with the deity for the benefit of an ancestor.

Finally, the verb occurs in the sense of recalling a person in thought in a fifth-century Aramaic text of Aḥikar (line 53): 'he will remember me and desire my counsel.'[5]

It is evident from these texts that we are dealing with a restricted usage of the verb due to the nature of inscriptional material. However, the usage is wide enough in scope to allow

---

[1]H. Torczyner, *The Lachish Letters, Lachish I*, (London, 1938), p. 37.

[2]G. A. Cooke, *A Text-Book of North-Semitic Inscriptions,* p. 83.

[3]C. F. Jean, Jacob Hoftijzer, *Dictionnaire des Inscriptions Sémitiques de L'Ouest* (Leiden, 1960), pp. 76 f.

[4]Cooke, *op. cit.,* p. 160. G. R. Driver, 'Problems in Aramaic and Hebrew Texts', *Analecta Orientalia* 12 (1935), p. 47, argues against Cooke and others that the verb *yzkr* in line 16 is also a pěʿal. This seems quite unlikely. There is only one example in the Old Testament of *zkr* in its simple stem with the noun *šēm*, while with the causative it is common.

[5]A. Cowley, *Aramaic Papyri of the Fifth Century* (Oxford, 1923), p. 221.

certain conclusions to be drawn. The verb reveals a pattern of usage closely paralleled to that of the Old Testament in which it signifies both a thought and an action. We conclude, therefore, that this usage of *zkr* is not unique to the Old Testament but indicates a common Semitic characteristic. Moreover, this usage would confirm the previous evidence that the question involved is one of semantic range rather than mental pattern.

However, another question immediately arises. Is this use of the verb 'remember' limited to the Semitic languages or is this a linguistic phenomenon found elsewhere? The writings of Homer offer a good point of departure. The Greek verb μιμνήσκομαι is the principle word used and occurs frequently with a wide range of meanings. It can mean simply to remember someone or something of the past (Iliad 24.4; 6.222). Also it occurs with the meanings to remind someone (Odyssey 3.103), to be mindful (Il. 7.371), and to mention (Od. 4.151). It also carries the meaning of remembering someone favourably (Od. 8.462; Il. 17.671), but without the forensic quality which is so prominent in Hebrew.

Several idioms occur in which the verb is used to denote an action. To remember one's father and mother means to take care of them (Od. 18.267); to remember rest is to go to sleep (Od. 16.481); to remember the evening meal is synonymous with preparing the supper (Il. 24.601); to remember the dead means to bury them (Il. 22.390). Moreover, there are two expressions which occur with great frequency in Homer and illustrate the same point. When the Achaeans 'think of battle' (μνήσαντο δὲ χάρμης), they again experience the lust for battle (Il. 4.222; 8.252). This response is often viewed as part of the actual combat (Il. 15.380). Again, there is the expression 'remember the shield of valour' μνήσασθε δὲ θούριδος ἀλκῆς (Od. 4.527; Il. 8.174; 11.566). The phrase occurs regularly in speeches of encouragement. When men remember their past victories, they are spurred on to renew the fighting.

Finally, there is an interesting parallel to the Old Testament in the Iliad (15.372 ff). Nestor offers a prayer to Zeus: 'remember these things, and ward from us the pitiless day of doom . . .'

Before summarizing the evidence from the use of the Greek verb, we turn briefly to analyse the Greek idioms employing the noun 'heart'. The heart does not occur idiomatically in Homer in parallelism with the verb 'to remember', as is common in Hebrew. However, the heart is commonly connected with the process of thought. The φρήν is the seat of the mental and emotional faculties, of perception and thought. The idiom differs slightly from that of Hebrew. It is not common to speak of objects or events rising on the heart or returning to the heart. Rather, the common expression is 'to place it in the heart' (βάλλειν, Il. 1.297; ποιεῖν, Il. 13.55; θέσθαι, Od. 14.227). Like Hebrew, one persuades or turns the heart toward an action (Il. 4.104).

The Greek idiom in Homer denotes both the process of thought as well as the action which follows. To set an idea in the heart is also to fix the path of action (Il. 9.600). Phoenix is alarmed that Achilles wants to 'set the homeward journey to his heart', because such will surely issue in action (Il. 9.434). The gods determine the acts of men by setting an idea in the heart of man which he in turn must execute (Il. 1.55; 4.104).

We should like now to summarize the evidence in Homer. Our purpose in turning to the Greek was to determine whether the usage of the verb 'remember' to signify both the process of thought and action which we established for Semitic was restricted to the Semitic family. The evidence is clear that Homeric Greek offers many close parallels both in the use of μιμνήσκομαι as well as in the idioms connected with the heart. We conclude, therefore, that no significant contrast can be made between Homeric Greek and the Semitic usage.

However, it would be a mistake in the light of this evidence to conclude that this usage of 'remember' was characteristic of all Greek writers.[1] There is an important change in usage which is reflected in the philosophical writings of Plato and Aristotle and which stands in marked discontinuity with the usage found in Homer.

The problem of Plato's use of memory (μνήμη) and recollection (ἀνάμνησις) is more complex than often realized. His use of μνήμη is not consistent throughout his writings. In the *Republic*

---

[1] A study of the New Testament's understanding of memory would necessitate another monograph. Cf. the fine beginning made by N. A. Dahl, *ST* 1 (1948), pp. 69 ff.

and *Phaedrus* it has a transcendental content while in the *Theaetetus* it seems to possess only empirical content.[1] Nevertheless, the clear assertion in *Philebus* 34a that 'memory may be rightly defined as the preservation of perception' indicates basically a different use of the term 'memory'. The word is restricted to a psychological process which relates to the apprehension of images and is separated sharply from the function of the will.

Aristotle goes to even greater effort to analyse the nature and function of memory in his treatise on 'Memory and Recollection'. According to him the process of remembering is confined to things of the past, not the present. He defines the act of remembering as 'the permanence of an image regarded as the copy of the thing it images . . .' (451a).[2] Memory depends on the retention of a sense stimulation after the object producing it has ceased to have an effect. Again, as in Plato, the act of remembering has been separated from external action, and confined to a psychological experience in relation to a neutral image.

The affect of the Greek philosophical understanding of the role of memory on the Christian tradition is especially manifest in the description of the nature of man by Nemesius of Emesa, written at the end of the fourth century AD.[3] His sophisticated analysis along the lines set by Plato employs words to describe the role of memory in a way which is quite foreign both to the Old Testament and Homer.

We are now ready to summarize. We began by agreeing with Barr's criticism that Pedersen's analysis of the Old Testament's concept of memory should be examined from the broader perspective of other relevant linguistic data. Our study showed that the characteristic manner in which the Old Testament uses the words related to memory cannot be restricted to Biblical Hebrew. Close parallels are found not only in North-west Semitic, but also in Homeric Greek. A different semantic value, however, was discovered in the Greek philosophical tradition of Plato and Aristotle.

[1]R. Cushman, *Therapei* (Chapel Hill, 1958), pp. 131, 133. Cf. for a further discussion of Plato's concept of memory F. M. Cornford, *Plato's Theory of Knowledge* (London, 1935), pp. 2 ff., 120 ff.

[2]G. R. T. Ross, *Aristotle: De Sensu and De Memoria* (Cambridge, 1906), p. 107.

[3]*A Treatise on the Nature of Man,* Library of Christian Classics IV (London, Philadelphia, 1955), pp. 339 ff.

The result of this study confirms Barr's contention that the issue is a semantic one and does not involve differing categories of thought. There is no real dichotomy between Greek and Hebrew mentality in respect to memory. The point is that the Old Testament, certain North-west Semitic inscriptions, and Homer share in assigning to the words of memory an unreflective, broad semantic value. This usage has been greatly restricted by the Greek philosophers because of their reflective, rational interests to denote only the mental process of recalling.

The Problem of 'Primitive' Mentality

Barr's final criticism concerns Pedersen's description of the 'primitive' character of the Hebrew language. Barr focuses on the linguistic problems involved and his argument is akin to that raised in the above paragraph regarding linguistic structure.

In our opinion, there is another problem involved in Pedersen's concept of the primitive character of Hebrew which is of equal importance. Pedersen seeks to reconstruct a type of primitive or prelogical mentality in which action is understood completely as a 'manifestation of the soul'.[1] Events, he maintains, not only form a unity with thought; they are actually created by the soul.[2] Whether an idea becomes an action is decided independently of external means by the quality of the soul.[3] The failure of an idea to become an event is a judgment on the soul of the originator of the idea. Event has become separated from the external world to become a reflection of the self.

Pedersen's analysis of primitive psychology rests in large measure upon such works as those of Grønbech[4] and Lévy-Bruhl.[5] Particularly the latter has advanced a comprehensive theory of a prelogical mentality. It lies beyond our present scope to attempt a full critique of Lévy-Bruhl's hypothesis. Enough criticism has been evoked from specialists in the field[6] to suggest that it is still

[1]Pedersen, *op. cit.*, p. 128. [2]*Ibid.*, p. 135. [3]*Ibid.*, p. 139.
[4]Vilhelm P. Grønbech, *Culture and Religion of the Teutons* (ET, London, 1931).
[5]L. Lévy-Bruhl, *Les Fonctions Mentales dans les Sociétés Inférieures* (9 ed., Paris, 1951); *La Mentalité Primitive* (14 ed., Paris, 1947).
[6]Cf. A. E. Jensen, *Mythos und Kult bei Naturvölkern* (2 Aufl., Wiesbaden, 1960), pp. 26 ff.; G. van der Leeuw, *De Primitieve Mensch en de Religie* (Groningen, 1952), pp. 5 ff.; P. Radin, *Primitive Man as Philosopher* (2nd rev. ed., New York, 1958), pp. 229 ff.

highly debatable to what extent such a prelogical mentality does actually exist among primitive peoples. Our present concern is whether Pedersen's analysis of Hebrew mentality is tenable.

Pedersen has attempted to point out aspects within the Old Testament's approach to psychology which distinguish it sharply from a modern approach. We agree with Pedersen's contention that certain elements of Old Testament thought show a similarity to the categories of thought which anthropologists find in contemporary primitive peoples. However, Pedersen's analysis has not fully recognized the important dislocations which Israel has effected in the pattern of prelogical thinking. The biblical evidence simply does not confirm his theory that event is conceived of merely as a manifestation of the soul and effected independently of external factors. The Hebrews were certainly aware that thoughts do not always lead to a corresponding action. This fact plays too obvious a role in human experience to have been ignored. In Num. 11.5 the Israelites in the desert complain to Moses: 'O that we had meat to eat. We remember the fish we ate in Egypt for nothing . . . and there is nothing at all but this manna to look at.' Quite obviously the thought of the Egyptian fish did not produce the desired results. To suggest that the thought produced the *act* of frustration does not alleviate the difficulty, since, according to the theory, the thought possesses the same content as the reality which it represents.

Or again, Mordecai admonishes Esther: 'Think not that in the king's palace you will escape any more than all the other Jews' (Esth. 4.13). Pedersen interprets this verse to mean that such a thought would not be a real thought, since it could not be put into effect.[1] But nowhere does the text suggest that the thought is less than real. A more obvious explanation is that Mordecai recognized a distinction between thought and action. These two examples are non-theological in character, and indicate that on the level of common experience Israel did not share consistently a prelogical mentality.

But one can go a step beyond this. Israel developed a sense of history because of its understanding of Yahweh's relation to the world which broke the primitive pattern. God controls the

[1]Pedersen, *op. cit.,* p. 126.

external world through the dimension of the historical. Joseph addresses his brothers: 'You intended evil against me; but God intended it for good' (Gen. 50.20). The evil plan of the brothers was thwarted not because of a weakness of their souls, but because God was working out his plan through the historical events. Again, Assyria thinks to destroy Jerusalem, but Yahweh plans to cut him down (Isa. 10.7 ff.). This concept of the significance of the historical event has no parallels in primitive societies. While Israel never developed its empirical sense after the manner of Aristotle, its recognition of the historical dimension of the external world shattered the framework of the so-called prelogical mentality.

To summarize: Pedersen's contribution lies in raising the problem of memory within the Old Testament and in analysing the range of meaning attached to the terms employed. He noticed especially that the Old Testament included under the verb *zkr* a range of actions wider than usually associated with the verb 'remember' in English.

However, James Barr's fundamental criticism of Pedersen's method as confusing a semantic problem with a theory of differing mentalities has been confirmed. The extra-biblical parallels seem conclusive at this point. Moreover, we feel that Pedersen's indiscriminate use of the categories of so-called prelogical thought has imposed a foreign category upon the Old Testament from the start. Event is more than an internal occurrence, reflecting the quality of the soul, but rather it is a unity of thought and action responding to the impulses of the outside world.

It is now our purpose to turn from the question of memory as posed by Pedersen, and attempt a form-critical analysis of the passages which employ the important words describing the role of memory. By discovering the context in which the terms were used within the life of Ancient Israel, we shall seek to discover the meanings attached to the words and trace any change in their employment.

III

GOD REMEMBERS

A. OCCURRENCE

THE verb *zkr*, used with God as subject, appears 73 times in the qal.[1] The occurrence of the verb is widely distributed throughout the whole Old Testament. There are, however, some significant omissions and concentrations. The verb is missing almost entirely in the JE strata, while it is a favourite expression of P. It appears infrequently in Deuteronomy and in the Deuteronomistic history. It is seldom employed by the prophets with the exception of Hosea and Jeremiah. The largest occurrence is in the Psalter. Finally, the word appears frequently in Nehemiah.

B. MEANING

The close agreement among the lexicons with regard to the basic meaning of the qal has already been pointed out. Still several problems remain. A closer examination of the syntactical relationship used in relating the verb to its object will help to bring the issues into focus.

There are various ways in which the verb relates itself syntactically to its object. The most frequent construction is with the direct object or with the preposition *lě*.[2] Of particular interest is the latter construction. It seems significant that the preposition appears only in relation to God's memory. What is the precise meaning of this phrase?

By and large, the preposition maintains its basic meaning of aiming toward a goal.[3] The emphasis falls on remembrance as an

[1] I Chron. 16.15 and Ps. 89.48 are to be emended according to the suggestion of *BH*, making God the subject of the verb. Conversely, Isa. 63.11 and Lam. 3.19 are to be emended so as to read Israel as the subject in both cases.

[2] The preposition *lě* occurs some 18 times in an adverbial relationship governing the genitive, and twice to express the accusative.

[3] Carl Brockelmann, *Hebräische Syntax* (Neukirchen, 1956), § 107a, pp. 99ff.

action directed toward someone rather than on the psychological experience of the subject. Moreover, the preposition has strong forensic overtones which appear in both a positive and negative sense. Nehemiah requests that God 'remember for good' all that he has done (5.19). The Psalmist pleads that God credit to David's account all his suffering (132.1). Similarly, Yahweh remembers in Israel's favour the devotion of her youth (Jer. 2.2). This is not a nostalgic reflection of Yahweh's, but rather a reckoning of this earlier loyalty to Israel's account.[1] Conversely, God can also remember in one's disfavour. It is accredited against Edom that it participated in the destruction of Jerusalem (Ps. 137.7). The Psalmist prays that the sins of the forefathers be not placed upon his account (79.8).

The evidence seems clearly to confirm a recent suggestion of H. J. Boecker[2] that *zākhār lĕ* is a technical term which bears a specific juridical meaning: to credit to one's account. The expression in its origin has its roots in the legal life of Ancient Israel and should be distinguished in meaning from the general sense of 'remember'. There is, however, an idiom which continues to carry the same strong forensic flavour without the use of the preposition. It is the expression 'to remember one's sins', in which case, 'in one's disfavour' is presupposed (cf. Isa. 43.25; 64.8; Jer. 14.10; Hos. 7.2; 8.13; 9.9; Ps. 25.7).

Boecker[3] suggests that the idea of Yahweh as judge lies at the root of the expression. This could explain why the term is restricted to Yahweh's remembering. The verb *zkr*, when referring to Israel's memory, almost never carries a forensic meaning. In the three examples where there is evidence of this the passages all deal with the relation of a subordinate to a superior (Gen. 40.14; I Sam. 25.31; II Sam. 19.20).

The evidence appears to confirm a forensic meaning in the above cases. In a recent article Reventlow[4] attempts to go far beyond this point. He defends the thesis that this meaning is not

[1] H. W. Wolff, 'Hauptprobleme alttestamentlicher Prophetie', *EvTh* 15 (1955), p. 461.
[2] H. J. Boecker, *Redeformen des israelitischen Rechtslebens* (Dissertation, Bonn, 1959), pp. 108 ff.
[3] *Ibid.*, p. 112.
[4] H. Graf Reventlow, 'Das Amt des Mazkir', *TZ* 15 (1959), pp. 161 ff.

to be restricted to certain idioms but that the verb itself has its roots in a legal setting. When the verb appears without a legal colouring, Reventlow insists that this shows a later stage in which the original meaning has been lost. However, in our opinion, his thesis frequently results in a strained interpretation and a failure to account for the full evidence.[1] The verb cannot be so restricted in meaning.

The discussion in chapter II revealed the wide semantic range of the verb *zkr* which included both the process of thought and the action. The parallelism of *zkr* with such verbs as *pqd* (appoint) indicates the objective character of the action comprehended in the verb (Pss. 8.5; 106.4). Frequently the psychological processes involved in remembering are included along with the purely objective action toward someone. God remembers and forgets and this process stands parallel to a series of psychological descriptions (Jer. 31.20; 44.21). Of course, God's remembering has not only a psychological effect, but an ontological as well. Whoever Yahweh does not remember has no existence (Ps. 88.6). When God forgets sin, he forgives (Jer. 31.34). Although in the majority of cases the subjective element is included, there are no examples where this reflection does not issue in the objective intervention toward that which was remembered. Memory is not identical with the action, but it is never divorced from it.

Although the objective side of God's memory is always present with varying emphasis, the importance of the subjective side should not be overlooked. Yahweh is reminded in the complaint psalm of the scorn of the heathen and the suffering of his people for the purpose of influencing and arousing his sympathy (Pss. 74.2, 22; 89.51). The intense emotional reaction of Yahweh's remembering Israel is well illustrated in Jer. 31.20: 'I do remem-

[1]The following reasons militate against Reventlow's thesis: (*a*) He fails to distinguish correctly between the qal and hiphil usages. As a result, he tends to impose the technical meaning of the hiphil on the qal. (*b*) The psychological aspects of *zkr* cannot be adequately dismissed as a later st   His attempt to explain the non-forensic usage as a loss of original mear unconvincing. Conversely, Ex. 13.3 and Josh. 1.13 hardly ref meaning. (*c*) The parallel verbs indicate that *zkr* is not to be forensically as suggested (cf. Ps. 74.22; Isa. 57.11). (*d*) The fre object clause cannot be adequately explained by his thesis Jer. 18.20; Ps. 78.39; Lam. 5.1).

ber him still. Therefore, my bowels yearn for him.' These violent emotions result in action toward Israel's redemption and do not merely linger in God's thoughts. There can be no dichotomy between God's thought and action.

To summarize: God's remembering always implies his movement toward the object of his memory. This action varies in nature, and can be physical or forensic. The objective side of memory is accompanied, in differing degrees, by an internal reaction on God's part. The essence of God's remembering lies in his acting toward someone because of a previous commitment.

C. FORM-CRITICAL ANALYSIS

The task of tracing the development of a term presents the exegete with a basic methodological decision. What is the proper method of approach? The method most frequently employed for a critical word study is to arrange the occurrences of the word in a chronological sequence according to literary sources, and then attempt to discover a development in usage. Many of the articles in Kittel's *Wörterbuch* are classic examples of this method. There are some obvious difficulties involved. How can one accurately trace the development of a term in a living oral tradition solely on the basis of chance occurrences on the literary level? Is there not danger that the artificial order of the literary sources be imposed upon material which may have another structure entirely?[1]

The form-critical approach, which has been developed with such precision in recent German Old Testament scholarship, attempts to avert these dangers by penetrating to the oral tradition. By examination of the form a word is set within the living context of an ancient institution. The task of a word study is to follow the development and change in meaning, not in an artificial isolation from the life of Israel, but within the larger framework of the history of the institution. This study will attempt to employ this critical method in tracing the development of the phrase 'God remembers'.

[1] Cf. G. von Rad's criticism of this method in *GSAT* (München, 1958), p. 238: 'If we want to go a step farther, instead of working with proof texts, it is necessary to throw light on the specific cultic tradition which lies behind the single statements and to arrange them from the point of view of the history of tradition.'

The verb with God as subject appears, first of all, in two very different forms. On the one hand, there is the imperative or jussive form of the verb imploring Yahweh to intervene (Pss. 74.18; 79.8). On the other hand, there is the finite verb in which confidence is expressed that Yahweh has already acted (Ps. 105.42), continues to act (Ps. 8.5), or will surely act in the future (Hos. 8.13). Moreover, these two forms correspond to two familiar patterns of Israel's cultic worship, namely, the complaint psalm and the hymn.

The Complaint Psalm

The structure of the complaint psalm has already been analysed so thoroughly as to make this unnecessary.[1] The complaint, whether individual or communal, opens with a direct appeal to God. The two most important features of this type are the complaint and the plea. The complaint presents in highly emotional language the cause of the psalmist's plight, while the plea expresses in a similarly passionate manner the request for Yahweh's aid. The usual form for the plea is the imperative, occasionally the jussive. Gunkel had already observed that a common formula of the plea is the expression 'remember'.[2]

A closer examination of the occurrence of the imperative confirms the suspicion that its provenance (*Sitz im Leben*) is the complaint psalm. The verb appears within the plea both in the individual complaint psalm (Ps. 25.6, 7; 119.49) as well as in the communal complaint (Pss. 74.2, 18, 22; 79.8; 106.4; 137.7; Isa. 64.8; Jer. 14.21; Lam. 5.1; Neh. 1.8). Its role appears in even sharper profile within the latter genre. The nature of the plea varies greatly with no fixed pattern within the predicate. The plea can be negative or positive: 'Do not remember against us the sins of our forefathers' (Ps. 79.8). 'Remember how the enemy scoff' (Ps. 74.18). The frequent appeal to the covenantal relationship indicates that the appeal to be remembered stems from Yahweh's

---

[1] W. Baumgartner, *Die Klagegedichte des Jeremia* (Giessen, 1917), pp. 6–27; H. Gunkel, J. Begrich, *Einleitung in die Psalmen* (Göttingen, 1933), pp. 117 ff., 172 ff.; C. Westermann, *Das Loben Gottes in den Psalmen* (Göttingen, 1954), pp. 35 ff., 44 ff.; 'Struktur und Geschichte der Klage im Alten Testament', *ZAW* 66 (1954), pp. 44 ff.

[2] Gunkel, *op. cit.*, p. 128.

earlier commitment to Israel (Jer. 14.21—*běrîth* (covenant); Ps. 25.6—*ḥesedh* (lovingkindness); Ps. 119.49—*dābhār* (promise); Ps. 74.2—*ʿēdhāh* (congregation).

The plight of the psalmist is often that of physical danger, but then again there are examples in which the forensic note dominates (Ps. 74.22). Still these elements are embedded within the complaint, and attempts to isolate a particular form out of the juridical sphere of life have not been successful.[1] In other words, the context is the cultic life and not the trial.

There are a few examples of the imperative appearing in early forms which are not, strictly speaking, complaint psalms, but are closely allied prayers. There are three examples of pleas within spontaneous prayers of individuals found in pre-exilic material. The prayer of Hannah has an obviously cultic setting, accompanied by a vow (I Sam. 1.11).[2] The prayer of Samson (Judg. 16.28) and Hezekiah (II Kings 20.3 = Isa. 38.3) are non-cultic in flavour. The form of the plea within these prayers is akin to that of the complaint psalm. Probably this common feature rests on an elemental quality of prayer as much as on the influence of a tradition.

Then again, the intercessory prayer is a form which shares many elements of the complaint.[3] Ex. 32.13 (cf. Deut. 9.27) is a good example of this type. Moses intercedes on Israel's behalf, addressing Yahweh in the vocative, followed by a typical complaint in which the words of the enemy are quoted. 'O Yahweh, why does thy wrath burn against thy people . . .? Why should the Egyptians say, "With evil intent did he bring them forth to slay them in the mountain"?' Then follows the plea: 'Remember Abraham, Isaac, and Israel . . .' There are several examples of the intercessory prayer directed specifically toward the king (Pss. 20.4; 89.48, 51; 132.1; II Chron. 6.42). Kraus has argued convincingly that an ancient 'royal Zion festival' lay at the root of these hymns.[4] This appears most clearly in Psalm 132. In the other

---

[1]Cf. Gunkel, Begrich, *op. cit.*, pp. 252 ff., in which they criticize the attempt to isolate a specific genre of prayer offered by the accused in H. Schmidt's *Das Gebet der Angeklagten im Alten Testament* (Giessen, 1928).

[2]A. Wendel, *Das freie Laiengebet im vorexilischen Israel* (Leipzig, 1932), pp. 105 f.

[3]F. Hesse, *Die Fürbitte im Alten Testament* (Dissertation, Erlangen, 1949).

[4]H.-J. Kraus, *Die Königsherrschaft Gottes im Alten Testament* (Tübingen, 1951), pp. 50 ff.; *Psalmen*, II (Neukirchen, 1960), pp. 879 ff.

examples the strong similarity to the complaint psalm would point to a period in Israel's history in which the festival had assumed the tone of sorrowful remembrance. 'O Lord, where is thy steadfast love of old, which by thy faithfulness thou didst swear to David? Remember how thy servant is scorned . . .' (Ps. 89.48, 51).

Up to this point the complaint has retained its original role within the cult and as a result has maintained its unbroken form. A major dislocation occurs once the form is adapted to a new environment which is detached from the original life of the cult. A most striking example of this process is found in the so-called 'confessions of Jeremiah', which because of their unique character will be treated apart from the general prophetic usage. Since the thorough examination by Baumgartner[1] no one has seriously questioned the relationship of the confessions to the complaint psalms. The older form has lost its cultic connection, and has been transformed into a dialogue between the prophet and Yahweh. The prophetic form retains the same intensity of expression, fluctuating between complaint and plea. But a strong mixture of prophetic material has entered in to fracture the earlier genre. Although traditional expressions appear in the complaint to describe the prophet's plight, the situation of the prophet is new. His isolation (15.17), rejection (15.15), desire for vengeance (18.21) stem from the unique role as bearer of the prophetic word (20.8 ff).[2] The confessions speak of physical pain, but this has become a figure for the prophet's spiritual shattering (15.18). His plea for Yahweh to remember refers to his special relation as prophet in a particular historical moment. 'Remember how I stood before thee to speak good for them' (18.20; cf. 15.15). But even more significant, the access to Yahweh's presence through the cult with the divine response has been replaced by a direct confrontation with Yahweh.

Job is likewise dependent upon the earlier form of the complaint psalm.[3] There are three examples of *zkr* addressing God in

[1]Baumgartner, *op. cit.*

[2]Cf. G. von Rad, 'Die Konfessionen Jeremias', *EvTh* 3 (1936), pp. 265–76. An important study from a different point of view is S. H. Blank, 'The Confessions of Jeremiah and the Meaning of Prayer', *HUCA* 21 (1948), pp. 331–54.

[3]F. Baumgärtel, *Der Hiobdialog, Aufriss und Deutung* (Stuttgart, 1933); C. Westermann, *Der Aufbau des Buches Hiob* (Tübingen, 1956), pp. 25 ff.

a plea and having a form which bears a strong resemblance to the traditional structure (7.7; 10.9; 14.13). However, the extent of deviation is even greater than that found in Jeremiah. His usage is characterized by a poetic freedom which allows him wide latitude. Westermann, following Bentzen, has analysed the author's usage of the complaint psalm as a 'dramatization' of the form.[1] The three traditional parts of the complaint psalm have been assigned to actual people as if in a drama. There is a question whether Westermann has been fully successful in attempting to interpret the entire book with this key. Nevertheless, his study has been fruitful in pointing up the problem of Job's adaptation of older material which has fully lost its cultic setting.

The content of Job's plea reflects a decidedly reflective tone. Frequent elements from ancient wisdom literature are introduced further to enrich his material (7.2). This does not imply that his pleas have sacrificed their note of urgency. His pleas turn on the transitory nature of human life. 'Remember that my life is a breath' (7.7). 'Remember that thou hast made me like clay' (10.9). In these examples the tremendous poetic creativity of the author transcends the traditional bounds of the psalm. Within almost infinite variety the writer takes up the thought of man's ephemeral nature and illustrates it with changing figures. His life is a breath . . . He vanishes before the eye . . . He fades as a cloud . . . He disappears into Sheol . . . He never returns to his home . . . His place has become unknown (7.7–10).

The imperative appears frequently in a stereotyped prose phrase in the book of Nehemiah (5.19; 6.14; 13.14, 22, 29, 31). The phrase, having almost the character of a gloss, is appended to the narrative without any real internal relation. Nehemiah pleads that his good deeds be accredited to his account and conversely that the evil deeds of his enemies be punished. At first sight one might consider this expression to be a final stage in the dissolution of the complaint psalm. However, it is more probable to see here the influence of another genre of literature which has no direct connection with the complaint psalm. Striking parallels to this formula have been found in Egyptian and Babylonian

[1] Westermann, *ibid.*, p. 9.

building inscriptions in which a plea is made to accredit the good deeds of the builder to his account.[1]

The prophetic oracle also shows a strong dependence on the cultic tradition of the complaint psalm. Recent Old Testament scholarship has continued to emphasize the deep roots of the prophetic message in the cultic tradition of Ancient Israel.[2] Yet the prophets were by no means cultic officiaries, nor was the cult the vehicle for their preaching. Their message came as a violent break with the tradition in which they themselves stood. The older forms have been taken up, then twisted into words of judgment, and hurled back into the faces of those who persisted in nurturing the sacred tradition of the past. The new use to which the complaint psalm has been put is a good illustration of this.

Hos. 6.11b–7.2 stands parallel to 6.4–6 in expressing Yahweh's reaction to the popular piety found in the priestly prayer of confession (6.1–3). The oracle, which is cast in the first person, fluctuates between sympathetic sharing of Israel's complaint and sharp denunciation of her wickedness. 'When I would restore the fortunes of my people, when I would heal Israel . . . they do not consider that I remember all their evil works.' The restoration of fellowship sought by Israel is categorically denied. Yahweh has found no covenantal loyalty (6.6); rather Israel's sins are 'before his face'. Similarly, Hos. 8.8, 11 ff. oscillates between threat and complaint.[3] In the midst of the prophetic invectives in vv. 11 and 13a, the divine complaint breaks forth in v. 12. *'attāh* (now, 13b) introduces the judgment: The covenant has been irrevocably broken. Israel will return to captivity in Egypt. Yahweh accredits her sins to her account (cf. 9.9).

Jeremiah 14 presents one of the most striking examples of the prophetic reaction to the tradition of the complaint psalm. Verses 2–6 describe the disastrous effect of a drought which calls forth a fast. Then follows the communal complaint in vv. 7–9. This is no

[1] Cf. R. Kittel, *Geschichte des Volkes Israel,* III (Stuttgart, 1929), p. 650; R. Bowman, *IB*, 3, p. 714.
[2] H. W. Wolff, 'Hauptprobleme alttestamentlicher Prophetie', *EvTh* 15 (1955), pp. 459 ff.
[3] H. W. Wolff, *Dodekapropheten* (BK, 14, Neukirchen, 1961), p. 173.

Canaanite liturgy, but echoes in each part ancient Yahweh tradition. Yahweh is addressed in the vocative, and implored to intervene with fervent pleas. A confession of guilt is made. Then plaintive cries of 'why', characteristic of the complaint, arise. Reasons are advanced why Yahweh should help. Israel is the covenant people, 'we are called by thy name' (v. 9). Yahweh has redeemed his people in the past, within a series of saving events: 'Redeemer in time of trouble' (v. 8). Yahweh dwells in Israel's midst (v. 9). The complaint ends with a last passionate cry: 'Leave us not!'

The divine answer comes in the form of an invective and threat (v. 10). Israel's prayer is not accepted. Her people can expect only judgment, because Yahweh 'remembers their iniquity'. A younger hand has elaborated on the judgment (vv. 11-12). The time of fasting and offering is over. The prophet must no longer intercede, because Israel now faces total destruction.

Finally, there is another adaptation of the complaint psalm equally as central for the prophetic message, which stands in the sharpest possible discontinuity with the above usage. Jer. 31.15-20 is composed of a series of separate units loosely joined together.[1] However, a discernible pattern is evident. Verse 15 introduces the bitter complaint of Rachel, the eponymic mother of the northern tribes, for her children who have been lost in exile. Verses 16-17 bring in response a word of promise from Yahweh that her children shall return. Then vv. 18-19 continue with another form of complaint, this time a prayer of repentance from Ephraim. Verse 20 is Yahweh's response which is given in a form closely akin to the salvation oracle (*Heilsorakel*): 'I do remember him still . . . I will surely have mercy on him.' Verse 20 has direct reference to Ephraim's prayer in v. 18, but also an indirect connection with Rachel's complaint in v. 15. Israel's complaint is not in vain; Yahweh will bring restoration.

It would be a grave mistake, however, to see in the prophetic word of promise an inconsistent weakening of the message of judgment and a mere return to an older, traditional form. This form has also been thoroughly transformed by its new content.

---

[1]Cf. R. Rendtorff, 'Zum Gebrauch der Formel *ne'um jahwe* im Jeremiabuch', *ZAW* 66 (1954), p. 33.

The reconciliation of Yahweh with Israel has not been accomplished within the structure of the cult. Rather, out of the despair of extinction (15.15) God has brought into being a new son relationship through mercy.

There are several other examples of the prophetic use of the verb 'remember' within the context of forgiveness. They occur, however, in passages which are not related to the complaint psalm. Isa. 43.25 assumes the form of a summons to a trial (*Appellationsrede*).[1] Jer. 2.2 reflects also a legal setting and is the speech of the defendant.[2] Jer. 31.34 is a promise which stems out of the ancient tradition of covenant renewal at a festival. These passages have in common the forensic usage of the verb which was discussed earlier. Israel's sins will not be accredited to her account.

The Hymn

The phrase 'God remembers' which employs a finite verb in the third person appears to have its original context within the structure of the hymn.[3] Its place is within the main body of the hymn in which Yahweh's great acts of the past are related in the perfect or narrative imperfect. One might have expected the phrase to have occurred in the individual thanksgiving psalm where the parallel with the complaint psalm would have been closer. Perhaps the use of the hymn relates to the fact that the object of God's memory in the psalms is never a single individual, but always the covenant people. The singular usage is confined to a few early prose narratives (Gen. 30.22; I Sam. 1.19).

The chief object of Israel's praise centres on Yahweh's faithfulness in remembering his covenant. 'He has remembered his covenant forever' (Ps. 105.8; cf. Ps. 106.45; 111.5; I Chron. 16.15). He has manifested toward Israel covenantal loyalty (Pss. 98.3; 106.45; 136.23). He continues to bless the house of Israel (115.12) and fulfil his word of promise to Abraham (105.42). Ps. 105.8, 42 views Israel's entire redemptive history as the result of God's remembering his covenant.

It is significant to observe that the object of God's memory

---

[1] J. Begrich, *ZAW* 58 (1940/41), p. 12; *Studien zu Deuterojesaja*, pp. 26 ff.
[2] H. J. Boecker, *op. cit.,* pp. 108 ff.
[3] H. Gunkel, *Einleitung in die Psalmen*, pp. 32 ff.

cannot be consistently confined to the past. The great acts of the covenant continue to meet Israel in her present situation. Ps. 111.5 speaks of the wonderful deeds of the past (*niphlā'ôth*) and draws the conclusion that 'he is ever mindful of his covenant'. Psalm 105 recounts the traditions of the redemptive history, but interprets this in v. 8: 'he is mindful of his covenant *forever*, of the word which he commanded for a *thousand generations*.' Similarly, Psalm 103 passes imperceptibly from the great acts of the Mosaic age (v. 7) to the contemporary memory of Israel's weakness (v. 14).

This evidence would seem to indicate that in terms of God's memory time-sequence plays a secondary role. How the great acts of the past relate to the present and the future is not seen as a problem which bears upon God's memory. His remembering is not conceived of as an actualization of a past event in history; rather, every event stems from the eternal purpose of God. Only from Israel's point of view is each remembrance past. God's memory is not a re-creating of the past, but a continuation of the selfsame purpose. According to the psalmist redemptive history does not end, because the present events which stem from God's memory are not different in quality from the former. God's memory encompasses his entire relationship with his people. His memory includes both the great deeds of the past as well as his continued concern for his people in the future.

The evidence points clearly to the fact that these hymns served a cultic end in Israel's worship. The Chronicler cites portions of Psalms 105 and 106 as belonging to the temple liturgy (I Chron. 16.15). The antiphonal character of Psalm 136 is obvious from the refrain. The same judgment applies to Psalm 115 in which changing voices within the liturgy can be observed (vv. 9–11). Moreover, general recognition of the cultic background of the royal hymns has steadily increased since Mowinckel's initial suggestion. We conclude that the phrase 'God remembers' reflects the cultic background of the hymn and parallels the imperative's role within the complaint psalm as part of Israel's worship.

Finally, the Priestly writer's usage of the term 'God remembers' at first seems closely related to that of the hymn. The form of the verb is always the finite verb and never the imperative. Moreover, the content of the memory is strikingly similar. The object of

God's remembering is either the recipient of the covenant (Noah, Gen. 8.1; Abraham, Gen. 19.29) or the covenant (*bĕrîth*) itself. In fact, of the 14 times in which *bĕrîth* appears with *zkr*, eight times occur within the Priestly circle (Gen. 9.15, 16; Ex. 2.24; 6.5; Lev. 26.42 [*tris*], 45). Ezek. 16.60 is a secondary passage, but closely allied to the Priestly writer.

In spite of these similarities, the strong discontinuities are even more striking. First of all, the setting of the phrase within the Priestly circle is completely uncultic in character. Instead, the formula has assumed a function within an historical work. The word appears in prose passages at key junctures in Israel's history of redemption. This is particularly interesting because the role of memory in the cult is not at all foreign to Priestly theology, as the use of *zikkārôn* (memorial sign) demonstrates. This aspect of the problem will be treated in chapter V.

Secondly, the phrase has become a highly developed theological term within the Priestly circles. The formula has severed its connection with the cult to assume a new role within a theology of history. For the Priestly writer Israel's history is covenantal history. As is well known,[1] the Priestly writer places his material within the framework of a series of covenants. History moves from the broad base of man's creation to a covenant with Noah which is reaffirmed with divine blessing after the flood, and finally focuses on God's eternal covenant with Abraham.[2] The covenant at Sinai comes as the completion of the fundamental relationship already established with Abraham. The use of the verb *zkr* reflects the Priestly writer's concern to present history as a witness to the unfolding of the purpose of the covenant God who is active in Israel's midst. This history is merely a working out of the one eternal act of divine grace.

Basic to the covenant were the specific promises to Abraham of a people and a land.[3] God's remembrance of his covenant to Moses included a renewed promise of the land (Ex. 6.8). Lev.

---

[1] Cf. G. von Rad, *Die Priesterschrift im Hexateuch* (Stuttgart, 1934), pp. 166 ff.; K. Elliger, 'Sinn und Ursprung der priesterlichen Geschichtserzählung', *ZTK* 49 (1952), pp. 121 ff.

[2] W. Zimmerli,, 'Sinaibund und Abrahambund', *TZ* 16 (1960), pp. 268 ff.

[3] Elliger, *op. cit.*, p. 129.

26.45 makes clear that remembering the covenant means possession of the land, but 26.42 insists on the pre-eminence of the Abrahamic covenant as the foundation of this hope.[1]

To summarize the final section: The verb used with God as the subject appears in two distinct formulae. On the one hand, the imperative form has its context within the complaint psalm. An expansion of the form away from its cultic origin was traced in the complaints of Jeremiah and Job. The great break came with the prophetic adaptation for purposes of judgment and promise. On the other hand, the use of the finite form of the verb arose within the hymn. The Priestly school accommodated the form to express a theological interpretation of covenantal history.

[1]Zimmerli, *op. cit.*, pp. 274–5.

IV

ISRAEL REMEMBERS

A. OCCURRENCE

THE qal form of the verb occurs 94 times.[1] The subject is usually Israel either as a people or as a member of a group. The verb occurs in the majority of cases with a direct object; however, in approximately ten examples it is followed by an object clause, and occasionally without any object. It is noteworthy that there is no instance of the verb with Israel as subject which subordinates its object by means of the preposition *lĕ*.

The distribution of the verb in the qal is particularly significant because of its high concentration in certain areas. The earliest strata of the Pentateuch are almost entirely missing. Three examples of E appear, all in the Joseph stories.[2] Num. 11.5 is usually assigned to J. There are only a few occurrences within the Priestly writings,[3] because the noun has apparently replaced the verb in importance (cf. ch. V). The verb occurs five times in the pre-exilic material of the historical books.[4] The entire corpus of pre-exilic prophecy also offers few examples.[5] Jeremiah at first seems to be an exception, but on closer examination of the five occurrences only one (20.9) is clearly pre-exilic.[6]

The first really significant concentration of occurrences falls in

---

[1]The following passages have been eliminated on textual grounds: I Chron. 16.15 and Ps. 89.48 (cf. *BH*). Ps. 77.12a should be read as a hiphil with the *kĕthîbh*. The text is corrupt in Nahum 2.6 (cf. *BH*). Conversely, the following passages have been added: Isa. 63.11 read *wayyizkĕrû* instead of the singular. In Lam. 3.19 read *zākhartî* instead of *zĕkhor*.

[2]Gen. 40.14, 23; 42.9.

[3]Num. 15.39, 40. Even here the emphasis is on the role of the tassels in evoking memory. In Ex. 20.8 only the motive clause can be ascribed to P.

[4]Judg. 9.2; I Sam. 25.31; II Sam. 14.11; 19.20; II Kings 9.25.

[5]Amos. 1.9; Micah 6.5; Isa. 17.10.

[6]The text is corrupt in 17.2. 51.50 is in the oracles against Babylon and is clearly exilic. 3.16 and 23.36 are controverted, but considered by most commentators later prose additions.

Deuteronomy with 13 examples, beside two which are found in the Deuteronomistic framework.[1] Within the Pentateuch Ex. 13.3 appears also to have been reworked by the Deuteronomist (cf. below). The verb occurs nine times in Ezekiel.[2] In the remaining post-exilic prophets there are only three other examples of the verb,[3] with the notable exception of Deutero-Isaiah in which there are nine occurrences.[4] The most frequent usage (17 ×) appears in the Psalter.[5] The verb continues to occur throughout the remainder of the Hagiographa with the highest frequency in Job, Ecclesiastes, and Lamentations.[6]

The objects of the verb fall into interesting categories. The most significant groups include the great acts of Yahweh (*circa* 22×), Yahweh himself (17×), his commandments (9×), sins (7×), special days (3×). In marked contrast with the usage with God as subject, nowhere does Israel remember the covenant (*bĕrîth*).[7] This is interesting, since Israel can forget the covenant (Deut. 4.23).

B. FORM-CRITICAL ANALYSIS

Once again the problem of methodology must be faced. A danger is present in feeling that the distribution of the verb offers a chronological framework along which the development of the term can be traced. However, instead of allowing the literary development to impose an artificial order, the attempt will again be made to penetrate to the oral tradition and to recover the living context out of which the word arose.

A form-critical study of the phrase 'Israel remembers' results

[1]Deut. 5.15; 7.18; 8.2, 18; 9.7; 15.15; 16.3, 12; 24.9, 18, 22; 25.17; 32.7; Josh. 1.13; Judg. 8.34.

[2]6.9; 16.22, 43, 61, 63; 20.43; 23.19, 27; 36.31.

[3]Jonah 2.8; Zech. 10.9; Mal. 3.22 (EVV: 4.4).

[4]Isa. 43.18; 44.21; 46.8, 9; 47.7; 54.4; 57.11; 63.11; 64.4. The plural should be read in Isa. 63.11.

[5]Pss. 22.28; 42.5, 7; 63.7; 77.4, 7; 78.35, 42; 103.18; 105.5; 106.7; 109.16; 119.52, 55; 137.1, 6; 143.5.

[6]Job 4.7; 11.16; 21.6; 36.24; 40.32 (EVV: 41.8); Prov. 31.7; Eccles 5.19; 9.15; 11.8; 12.1; Lam. 1.7, 9; 3.19 (cf. *BH*), 20; Esth. 2.1; Neh. 4.8 (EVV: 14); 9.17; I Chron. 16.12 = Ps. 105.5; II Chron. 24.22.

[7]Pss. 103.18 and 106.7 offer the closest approximation to the idea. The term *bĕrîth* does appear in Amos 1.9, but with reference to Tyre's covenant with Edom.

in an analysis which differs greatly from that of the phrase 'God remembers'. Whereas the latter expression appeared within a fixed cultic context, the former shows no such uniformity. In fact, the tremendous variety in the use of the phrase within every conceivable genre clearly gives evidence that the term did not have its origin within any one prescribed area of Israel's life, such as the cultic or legal sphere. Rather, the verb when used with Israel as its subject denotes a basic human psychological function: to recall a past event.

(1) The verb appears in narrative from the earliest period to the latest in Israel's history with this basic psychological meaning. 'Joseph remembered the dreams which he had dreamed' (Gen. 42.9). '(King Ahasuerus) . . . remembered Vashti' (Esth. 2.1). It appears in the imperative (II Kings 9.25) as well as in a variety of indicative forms. Occasionally it appears in narrative with the secondary meaning of 'remember in one's favour' (I Sam. 25.31) and even carries a certain forensic overtone (II Sam. 19.20).

(2) The verb occurs within the legal material of the Pentateuch. Frequently it is attached to another verb to form the familiar Hebrew idiom 'remember to do' the commandments (Num. 15.39, 40). The verb has a paranetic function and bears the same non-technical meaning as above. This is especially true in the Deuteronomic preaching (Deut. 15.15; 24.9, 18, etc.). It is also true in the much more controverted passage in the Decalogue (Ex. 20.8): 'Remember the Sabbath to keep it holy.' Recent scholarship has tended more and more to recognize the extremely early character of this apodictic series.[1] However, the fact of a later reworking is also recognized. The form of v. 8 does not follow the earliest, apodictic formulation which would perhaps read: 'You shall not do work on the Sabbath' (*lōʾ taʿăśeh mĕlāʾkhāh bāššabbāth*).[2] The subsequent motive clause for Sabbath observation bears the stamp of the Priestly writer and reflects Gen. 1.1–2.3.[3]

[1] Cf. the most recent work of J. J. Stamm with full bibliography, *Der Dekalog im Lichte der neueren Forschung* (Bern, 1958).

[2] A. Alt, *Kleine Schriften zur Geschichte des Volkes Israel*, I (München, 1953), pp. 317 f.; K. Rabast, *Das apodiktische Recht im Deuteronomium und im Heiligkeitsgesetz* (Berlin, 1948), pp. 35 ff.

[3] Cf. Ernst Jenni, *Die theologische Begründung des Sabbatgebotes im Alten Testament* (Zürich, 1956), pp. 5 ff.

What can be said about the meaning of *zākhôr* (remember) in this passage? The marked uncultic character of the Decalogue has long been noted. This characteristic indicates its particular function within Israel rather than an alleged stage of religious development. Modern Old Testament research has been almost unanimous in its emphasis on the cult as the bearer of the Sinai tradition.[1] The Decalogue had its provenance within a covenant renewal ceremony. Nevertheless, the content of the commands were directed to the secular, everyday life of the people and not to the priests.[2] The Sabbath is the only festival mentioned, yet it is precisely the one which demands a non-cultic observance. It is sanctified by rest. Because it is not distinguished cultically from the other days, particular care must be taken to maintain its observance. 'Remember' does not carry a technical sense; rather, it is a paranetic term calling for the people to be aware of this special day in such a way as to set it apart from the ordinary days of the week.

(3) The verb plays a role within two closely allied forms, the trial (*rîbh*) and the disputation.[3] Begrich has pointed out the differing backgrounds of these two forms. The former arises out of a strictly legal setting, while the latter stems from any disagreement between members of the community. Yet in practice the two are often difficult to distinguish. The appeal to memory has a similar function in the two forms. The accused in a trial defends himself against the accusations levelled against him by appealing to his

---

[1]S. Mowinckel, *Le Décalogue* (Paris, 1927), pp. 114 ff.; A. Alt, *Kleine Schriften*, I, pp. 216 ff.; G. von Rad, *Das formgeschichtliche Problem des Hexateuch*, in *GSAT*, pp. 28 ff.; W. Zimmerli, 'Ich bin Jahwe', *Geschichte und Altes Testament* (Tübingen, 1953), pp. 206 ff.; W. Kessler, *VT* 7 (1957), pp. 1 ff.

[2]G. von Rad, *Theologie des Alten Testaments*, I (München, 1957), pp. 194 f. Cf. ET with revisions (Edinburgh, 1962), pp. 193 ff.

[3]For a discussion of these types, cf. the following literature: J. Begrich, *Studien zu Deuterojesaja*, pp. 19 ff., 42 ff.; B. Gemser, 'The *rîb*- or controversy pattern in Hebrew mentality', *Wisdom in Israel and in the Ancient Near East*, ed. M. Noth and D. Winton Thomas (*VT* Supplement 3, Leiden, 1955), pp. 120 ff.; H. J. Boecker, *Redeformen des israelitischen Rechtslebens*; E. Pfeiffer, 'Die Disputationsworte im Buche Maleachi', *EvTh* 12 (1959), pp. 546–68; G. E. Wright's article on Deut. 32 in the memorial volume for J. Muilenburg ('The lawsuit of God', in *Israel's Prophetic Heritage*, ed. B. W. Anderson and W. Harrelson, New York, London, 1962).

former action. Micah 6.3–5 is a classic example. Yahweh defends himself against Israel's charges by referring to his acts of redemption in the past. Deut. 32.6–7 is another occurrence of the *ríbh* in an expanded form. There are no good examples of a pure disputation form occurring with the verb *zkr*, but later prophetic employment of the form suggests a similar usage (cf. Isa. 46.8, 9; 57.11).

(4) Again the verb plays a role within a wide variety of cultic forms. It appears in the hymn calling forth Israel's thankful remembrance of the great acts of the past (Ps. 105.5 = I Chron. 16.12). Frequently in the complaint psalm the psalmist, recalling an earlier and happier experience, breaks forth in complaint and plea (Pss. 42.5; 137.1). Conversely, the individual thanksgiving psalm recounts the role which the remembering of Yahweh had in the deliverance (Jonah 2.8 [7]). Moreover, the verb appears in psalms of trust (Ps. 119.52, 55) as well as imprecatory psalms (Ps. 109.16).

There is another form of psalm which has not as yet been adequately investigated, but one in which *zkr* plays a key role. Psalms 78 and 106, Isa. 63.7 ff. and Neh. 9.16 ff. have in common not only a recitation of Yahweh's great acts of redemption, but also a history of Israel's disobedience in response to these events. Because Israel did not remember what Yahweh had done, she was rebellious. Of course, there are early roots in this development. The Deuteronomic preaching had often pointed out Israel's record of disobedience in failing to remember (Deut. 9.7), and the Deuteronomistic editor had used it as a framework for his history (Judg. 8.34). But the psalmist has employed the pattern for cultic usage. Nehemiah 9 clearly portrays a fast with a ceremony of public confession. A similar usage is reflected in Psalm 106 and Isa. 63.7 ff. Psalm 78 shows a somewhat different function. The motif of rebellion has been used within the Zion tradition to legitimatize the rejection of Ephraim and the choice of David.

(5) Turning to the prophets the evidence once again confirms the thesis that the verb *zkr* is not at home in any one given circle of tradition. Almost every conceivable prophetic form finds use for the verb without any discernible technical formulae. The following forms appear:

(*a*) Warning (*Mahnwort*), Isa. 44.21; Jer. 51.50; Mal. 3.22 (EVV: 4.4)

(*b*) Invective (*Scheltwort*), Amos 1.9; Isa. 17.10; Ezek. 16.22; 23.19

(*c*) Taunt (*Spottlied*), Isa. 47.7

(*d*) Disputation (*Disputationswort*), Isa. 46.8, 9; Isa. 57.11

(*e*) Trial (*Gerichtsrede*), Micah 6.5; Ezek. 16.43

(*f*) Salvation Oracle (*Heilsorakel*), Isa. 43.18; 54.4

(*g*) Promise (*Verheissungswort*), Isa. 65.17; Zech. 10.9; Ezek. 6.9; 16.61, 63; 20.43; 36.31

(*h*) Threat (*Drohwort*), Ezek. 23.27.

(6) Finally, the verb with a human subject appears in wisdom sayings: Prov. 31.7; Eccles 5.19; 11.8; 12.1.

C. THEOLOGICAL DEVELOPMENT

Up to this point our analysis indicates that the verb when used with a human subject did not originally have a technical meaning attached to it from a specific cultural context. Rather, the word was employed with its basic psychological sense in many different situations. Now it is necessary to go a step farther. Is there any evidence to show that the verb assumed a new meaning which went beyond the general psychological? We feel that there is such evidence and suggest the following thesis: A new and highly theological usage of *zkr* emerged from Israel's attempt to reinterpret the significance of her tradition.

(1) In the preaching of the Deuteronomist the word is used with a theological significance which goes beyond the general psychological. The word occurs with a high enough frequency to yield positive results in exegesis.

We start our investigation with Deut. 8.2: 'and you shall remember all the way which Yahweh your God has led you.' The appeal to remember is set within a typical Deuteronomic paranesis. The hortatory framework of vv. 1 and 6: 'keep the commandments', sets the purpose of the discourse. Verse 2 places v. 1 within its proper context as covenant history. The claims of Yahweh upon Israel cannot be properly understood apart from

50

historical memory. The commandments are not expressions of abstract law, but are events, a part of God's redemptive history toward Israel. Present Israel stands in an analogous situation with the people of the Exodus. Israel is still being tested. The covenant history of Yahweh with his people continues. The role of Israel's memory here is not to relive the past, because much of what is remembered is painful, but to emphasize obedience in the future. Memory serves to link the present commandments as events with the covenant history of the past.

The commandments of v. 1 are given to the covenant people. Israel does not become the covenant people by fulfilling the law. She has already been redeemed. Her present obedience to the commandments has only redemptive significance as part of this covenant history. The commandments given to a former generation continue to lay claim anew on each generation. Yet one cannot separate instruction in the law from covenant history. In this passage historical memory establishes the continuity of the new generation with the decisive events of the past. God's plan for Israel unfolds in her history. As in the past, Israel's history continues to be God's forcing his people to decide between life and death.

The Deuteronomist takes up the ancient promise of the land sworn to the patriarchs which occurs in an unconditional form in the Pentateuch,[1] but puts it now within a conditional framework. Only when Israel is obedient to the claims of the Mosaic covenant will the promise be fulfilled. Memory plays a central role in making Israel constantly aware of the nature of God's benevolent acts as well as of her own covenantal pledge.

A similar usage of memory in establishing the continuity between the past covenantal history and the present appears in the following passages: 7.18; 9.7; 24.9; 25.17. Israel remembers what Yahweh once did to Pharaoh and Egypt. Yahweh will do so again to Israel's present enemies (7.18). Israel must not forget that Yahweh has given her land in spite of her rebellion. Israel should remember that she acted as a rebellious people in the past and still is stubborn (9.6 ff.). While there is no attempt in these

---

[1] G. von Rad, 'Verheissenes Land und Jahwes Land im Hexateuch', *GSAT*, pp. 87 ff.

passages to renew past history, Israel's memory does serve a far more important role than merely providing illustrations from the past. It serves in making Israel noetically aware of a history which is ontologically a unity. There is only one redemptive history.

There is a second usage of *zkr* in Deuteronomy which presents a different form as well as meaning. The passages in question are 5.15; 15.15; 16.12; 24.18, 22. The stereotyped form is at once apparent. Each passage begins with a command regarding some specific command.[1] This is followed in every case with the phrase: 'You shall remember that you were a slave in Egypt' (*wĕzākhartā kî-ʿebhedh hāyîthā bĕʾereṣ miṣrayim*). In three instances this central portion is further expanded with a waw consecutive imperfect which introduces the deliverance (*wayyîṣʾākhā*, 5.15; *wayyiphdĕkhā*, 15.15; 24.18). The final portion reiterates the original commandment. In four cases it is introduced by the adverb 'therefore' (*ʿal-kēn*). The waw consecutive in 16.12 carries the same force. Jenni notices the problem of the verb *wĕzākhartā* (you shall remember) being so closely linked both to what precedes (5.14b, the freeing of slaves from work) and to what follows (15b, the redemption from Egypt) that it is difficult to decide the priority of connection.[2] A form analysis, however, would seem to point to a primary connection with that which precedes, because the phrase in 15b is missing in some of the parallel passages. Nevertheless, Jenni is certainly right in seeing a close-knit unity of thought between both parts.

We now turn to 5.15. The Sabbath command of Deuteronomy differs in several important features from Ex. 20.8. Our concern will focus on the usage of *zkr* in the formulation of the command, and the differing motive clauses. First of all, how does Israel's memory of her slavery relate to the command to keep the Sabbath? The syntactical structure of the sentence makes it clear that Israel's memory of her own slavery (v. 15a) does not act as the motivation for allowing slaves to participate in the Sabbath observance. This frequent interpretation fails to explain the

---

[1] There is no uniformity in its present form, but the prohibitive, apodictic commands in 15.15 and 24.18 seem closest to the original.

[2] Jenni, *op. cit.*, p. 17.

'therefore' (*'al-kēn*) of v. 15b.[1] Memory does not serve to arouse a psychological reaction of sympathy for slaves. Rather, quite the reverse is true. Israel observes the Sabbath *in order to* remember her slavery and deliverance. This connection is made even more explicit in 16.3: 'You shall eat no unleavened bread . . . *in order that you may remember* (*lĕma'an tizkōr*) the day you came out of Egypt.' The festival arouses and incites the memory.[2]

Jenni has observed with genuine perception that 'according to the Deuteronomist the remembrance of the redemption out of slavery in Egypt provides the basic reason why the Sabbath is celebrated at all'.[3] The Deuteronomist's concern is not primarily humanitarian, but theological. He is concerned that 'all Israel' participate in the Sabbath.[4] This is only a reality when the slaves also participate. Israel's memory functions to assure the proper celebration of the Sabbath by remembering the nature of the Sabbath in Egypt at the time of the Exodus. Memory has a critical function of properly relating the present with the past. This critical role is confirmed by its frequent parallelism with the verb *byn* (discern, consider, Deut. 32.7; Isa. 43.18, etc.). The role of memory as a test of the existing cult in the light of the past historical tradition differentiates it sharply from the mythical in which the past is harmonized to conform to the present.

There is another aspect of memory in this same verse. When Israel observes the Sabbath in order to remember the events of her redemption, she is participating again in the Exodus event. Memory functions as an actualization (*Vergegenwärtigung*) of the decisive event in her tradition. The sign of the continuing relationship

---

[1]It is instructive to contrast the syntax of Ex. 20.8 ff. with that of Deut. 5.12 ff. In Ex. 20 the 'therefore' clause of 11b results from the previous indicative statement in 11a. Yahweh rested and as a consequence he blessed. This is not the case in Deut. 5. V. 15 is co-ordinated, not subordinated to 14b. The 'therefore' clause does not result from a previous indicative statement; rather, v. 15 clearly carries an imperative force followed by an object clause.

[2]Contrast this Deuteronomic formula with the several passages in which causal, often psychological connection is made between Israel's slavery and a commandment (Ex. 23.9; Lev. 19.34; Deut. 10.19; 23.8). The form of all these passages is similar, with *kî* introducing a causal clause. Significantly, the verb *zkr* is always missing.

[3]Jenni, *op. cit.*, p. 17.

[4]G. von Rad, *Das Gottesvolk im Deuteronomium* (Stuttgart, 1929), pp. 37 ff.

of Yahweh to his people is the rest of the Sabbath. Israel in every generation remembers and so shares in the same redemptive time.

This latter function of memory seems directly related to mythical thinking in which the determinative act of the past is renewed yearly in the cultic drama. However, the Deuteronomic parallels to 5.15 indicate the extent to which the older cultic pattern has been significantly altered. Sabbath observance (5.12 ff.) and the feast of weeks (16.9 ff.) have become, along with their non-cultic parallels (15.12 ff.; 24.17 ff., 19 ff.), merely examples of obedient response to the divine commandments. Memory as an act of actualization is not an automatic cultic rite, but occurs in the faithful response to the claims of the covenant. Deuteronomy has secularized the older cultic pattern in substituting a broad theological basis for cultic recital.

It is a natural development in thought when the Deuteronomist uses the verb in the sense of 'to act in obedience toward'. 'Remembering Yahweh' in 8.18 is contrasted in v. 19 with 'forgetting him', which is 'to go after other gods and serve them and worship them'. Joshua exhorts the people to 'remember the word which Moses commanded you' (Josh. 1.13). The people answer in v. 16: 'All that you have commanded us we will do . . . Just as we obeyed Moses . . . so we will obey you.'

There is one final Deuteronomic passage to discuss. Most commentators have been in agreement since Wellhausen's analysis that Ex. 13.3–10 bears the stamp of a Deuteronomic reworking of an older account.[1] The idiom is clearly that of D, but the awkward change in number would indicate that the content is no free creation of the writer. To what extent does the passage reflect the theology of Deuteronomy?

We suggest that there is a close parallel to the form which we have just discussed. 'Remember this day in which you came out from Egypt . . . therefore, no leavened bread shall be eaten'

[1] It is becoming increasingly clear that D cannot always be distinguished from E. Both arose out of North Israelite circles (cf. G. E. Wright, *IB*, 2, pp. 319 f.). However, in this case, the palimpsest effect of the passage, with the later reworking exhibiting such obvious signs of the Deuteronomistic style, militates against assigning the passage to E. Cf. Baentsch, *Exodus, Leviticus, und Numeri* (Göttingen, 1903) *ad loc.*, for a thorough analysis of the style.

(Ex. 13.3). The only section missing is the initial exhortation to keep the festival of unleavened bread. The object of Israel's memory is not the festival, but the day of redemption as in the Sabbath command. The waw consecutive which introduces the final clause carries the same force as the waw in Deut. 16.12. A closer examination of the whole passage explains the change in the structure. The writer is trying to maintain a distinction between the first observance in Egypt and the subsequent festival. Only after Israel enters the promised land is the festival established. Then the typical imperative is given: 'You shall keep this service in this month' (Ex. 13.5). If one recognizes the artificial character of this distinction, it becomes apparent that memory plays the same role here as it does in the theology of Deuteronomy which we discussed above. In the festival Israel remembers her tradition and thus actualizes it.

Moreover, it is precisely this concept of memory which is reflected in the rest of the passage (Ex. 13.3–10). Verse 5b: 'Keep this service'; v. 9: 'It is a memorial (*zikkārôn*) . . . that the Torah is in your mouth'; v. 10: 'Therefore keep this ordinance from year to year.' The festival of unleavened bread serves as a reminder to future generations of Yahweh's law. The role of memory has been completely reversed by the Deuteronomist.

The Deuteronomic parallel to Ex. 20.8, Deut. 5.12, reads 'keep' (*šāmôr*) in place of 'remember' (*zākhôr*). Some commentators feel that this difference is inconsequential. However, the evidence would seem to indicate that the change is part of a larger pattern. We would like to argue that the formula of Ex. 20.8 is primary and that because of a particular theology of remembrance, the Deuteronomist has substituted *šāmôr*. Israel does not remember festivals, but observes them in order to remember.

We shall briefly summarize the Deuteronomic usage. The writer has as his chief problem the relating of the new generation of Israel to the tradition of Moses. No longer has Israel direct access to the redemptive events of the past. Now memory takes on central theological significance. Present Israel has not been cut off from redemptive history, but she encounters the same covenant God through a living tradition. Memory provides the link between past and present. The Deuteronomist is acutely aware that Israel's redemptive history has not ceased. Her history continues only as present Israel established her continuity with the past through memory. The divine commands as event meet each successive generation through her tradition calling forth a decision, and in obedience Israel shares in the same redemption as her forefathers.

(2) Within the pre-exilic prophets the only significant change in meaning from the common untheological usage is found in Micah 6.5. The form of the unit in which this verse appears is that of the trial. The controversy of Yahweh with his people receives its familiar cosmological background with the summons to the mountains and hills to participate (cf. Isa. 1.2; Micah 1.2). Yahweh as the accused defends himself in the first person. Using the typical form of self-defence he refers Israel to his past dealings with her by reviewing her redemptive history. 'I brought you up from the land of Egypt, and redeemed you from the house of bondage.' The climax of the defence comes in the appeal: 'Remember . . . what happened on the way from Shittim to Gilgal that you may know the saving acts (*ṣidhqôth*) of Yahweh.'[1]

Boecker has shown that the appeal to memory is characteristic of a defendant's speech.[2] The accused attempts to demonstrate from the past that he is not guilty of the wrong of which he is charged. Yet it is apparent that in this passage the verb *zkr* has received a meaning in respect to Israel's past tradition which differs greatly from the typical usage within a trial. Israel must remember 'to know the saving acts of Yahweh'. The act of remembering serves to actualize the past for a generation removed in time from those former events in order that they themselves can have an intimate encounter with the great acts of redemption. Remembrance equals participation. The present rupture in the relationship of Yahweh with his people stems from Israel's failure to understand the saving acts.

[1]Cf. the standard commentaries for the textual and literary problems in vv. 4–5. For 5c several similar emendations have been proposed. Read with Weiser *bĕꜥobhrĕkhā* in place of *bĕꜥôr*. The names in 4b may have been secondarily added. Cf. H. Wildberger, *Jahwes Eigentumsvolk* (Zürich, 1960), p. 60. For a discussion of the Balaam traditions, cf. M. Noth, *Überlieferungsgeschichte des Pentateuch* (Stuttgart, 1948), pp. 80 ff.

[2]Boecker, *op. cit.*, p. 106.

In a recent study of this passage W. Beyerlin[1] has defended the view that Micah is dependent in large measure upon earlier cultic traditions of the Exodus. A comparison with Joshua 24 indicates a common cultic structure as well as cultic content. However, Beyerlin will go one step farther. He suggests that the verb *zkr* is a technical cultic term which has as its role the actualization of the redemptive acts within the cultic festival.[2] We do not agree with this latter thesis and feel that the arguments advanced are not tenable.[3] However, in spite of this disagreement, Beyerlin's actual interpretation of the passage is very close to our own. There is a cultic flavour present because Yahweh has taken up Israel's sacred tradition and repeats the redemptive history now in his own defence. Beyerlin paraphrases the prophet's message to the people as follows: 'In your worship you nourish the memory of Yahweh's redemptive acts. Now try *really* to remember them for once . . .'[4]

Yahweh's defence is an implicit protest against Israel's cultic system. Precisely in these redemptive acts (*ṣĕdhāqoth*) he has revealed his righteousness (*ṣĕdhāqāh*). But Israel has no understanding; she does not 'know'. In order to participate in this redemption, a righteous response is demanded. Micah's polemic is against a cult which continues to thrive as the bearer of Israel's sacred tradition, while at the same time tolerating the worst possible convenantal abuses within the life of the people (cf. 2.1 ff.; 3.1 ff.; 9 ff.; 6.6 ff., 9 ff.). The prophet appeals to Israel's memory as a means of actualizing Yahweh's original purpose for his people.

---

[1]W. Beyerlin, *Die Kulttraditionen Israels in der Verkündigung des Propheten Micha* (Göttingen, 1959), pp. 69 ff.

[2]*Ibid.*, pp. 70 f. A similar position is taken by H. Gross, 'Zur Wurzel ZKR', *BZ* 4 (1960), pp. 321 ff.

[3]The following reasons, in our opinion, contradict Beyerlin's thesis that *zkr* is here a technical cultic term: (*a*) Our form-critical study showed no evidence that the verb with Israel as the subject was ever a technical cultic expression. Only occasionally does it appear within a cultic framework and then without a technical meaning (Ps. 105.5). (*b*) The setting in Micah 6.1–5 is legal, as Boecker has demonstrated. (*c*) The cultic use of the noun *zĕkher* (name) cannot be cited as proof. As ch. V points out, the noun is related to the hiphil form of the verb and not the qal. It does not play the role of actualizing the past.

[4]Beyerlin, *op. cit.*, p. 71.

(3) Again Deutero-Isaiah employs the verb *zkr* in a way which goes far beyond the general psychological meaning. To be sure, many passages continue to carry the general psychological meaning within a variety of forms. Israel recalls with regret the glorious days of the past (63.11). In an oracle of promise the prophet foresees a time when she will not 'hold in mind' her former shame any more (54.4). The verb occurs again with the meaning 'to be aware of' and is parallel to the expression 'to place upon the heart' (47.7; 57.11). In 64.4 the meaning has shifted to signify an 'acknowledging' or 'turning to' Yahweh.

However, there is another series of passages in Deutero-Isaiah which goes far beyond this general sense and bears the particular stamp of his eschatological hope. The problem is set by an exiled people who try vainly to relate themselves to a former covenant history. The prophet exhorts the people in 46.9: 'remember the former things of old for I am God . . . declaring the end from the beginning.' The 'former things' are here not specific historical deeds, but rather include the entirety of God's past dealings with Israel.[1] These former things point to God's sovereignty over history. He is bringing to pass his purpose (*ḥēpheṣ*), which spans both the beginning and end of history. By linking herself to the past in memory Israel becomes part of the future, because past and future are one in God's purpose. J. Muilenburg comments poignantly on this passage: 'Thus historical memory and the oneness of God are joined.'[2]

A similar concept of memory and history appears in Isa. 44.21 which refers back most probably to vv. 6–8. Yahweh, who is Israel's redeemer, is 'first and last'. Because of his absolute control over history, he can announce his will in the past and accomplish it in the future. Israel is his witness. Again v. 21 does not refer to specific incidents within history, but to a faith reality which embraces all of history and calls forth Israel's response.

In the light of these verses, it comes as a surprise to read in

---

[1] For a survey of the exegetical problems involved, cf. C. R. North, 'The "Former Things" and the "New Things" in Deutero-Isaiah', in *Studies in Old Testament Prophecy*, ed. H. H. Rowley (Edinburgh, 1950), pp. 111 ff.; A. Bentzen, 'On the Ideas of "the old", and "the new" in Deutero-Isaiah', *ST* 1 (1948), pp. 183–7.

[2] Muilenburg, *IB*, 5, p. 541.

43.18 of an admonition which seems to be its direct antithesis: 'Do not remember the former things, nor consider the things of old.' Yet when read in context, this verse differs only in emphasis and, in fact, stems from a similar eschatological hope. The prophet warns an Israel seeking continuity and meaning in her existence not to turn to the former things. God is doing a new thing which is so great as to overshadow the past completely. God's redemption of Israel in history can be experienced by looking to the future rather than looking to his former deeds. This similar contrast occurs in 65.17 in terms of the new heavens.

The prophet stresses both the continuity and the discontinuity of history. There is a continuity between the past and the future because of the one purpose of God. There is a discontinuity because of Israel's failure. Israel's past response evokes the need of a radically new quality within history. In both instances Israel's memory is an active response in faith which links her to the redemptive action of God's entrance into history.

(4) Ezekiel focuses his attention on the problem of Israel's remembering her sins. Three times the object of memory is the 'days of her youth'. The phrase can refer to an early shame and subsequent rescue so that not to remember them is to be ungrateful (16.22). Or the early days can be sinful days which are not to be remembered (23.19, 27). When Israel remembers her sinful ways, she loathes herself (16.61; 20.43; 36.31). Likewise, the effect of Israel's remembering Yahweh is to loathe the sin into which she has fallen (6.9; 16.63).

There is another feature in Ezekiel's use of the term 'remember' which is even more striking. The verb is connected consistently with the formula: 'they (or you) shall know that I am Yahweh' (6.10; 16.62; 20.44; 36.23). Zimmerli has pointed to a special prophetic form which appears frequently in an expanded state in Ezekiel. The prophet announces an event which has as its function the self-revelation of Yahweh's nature (*Erweiswort*).[1] The knowledge of God stems from an act of his in history. It is in no sense a process of human speculation on the essence of God, but

[1] W. Zimmerli, 'Das Wort des göttlichen Selbsterweises (Erweiswort), eine prophetische Gattung', *Mélanges Bibliques rédigés en l'honneur de André Robert* (Paris, 1957), pp. 154–64.

remains a response to the divine initiative. Zimmerli correctly emphasizes that Israel's response in acknowledging these acts of God is not a secondary knowledge of second-rate importance in comparison with the original events of Sinai, but a completely new actualization.[1]

The verb *zkr* comes to mean a recognition or discernment which turns one toward God. Zimmerli defines it as a 'genuine reaching out after a reality, which in the very act becomes a new and living present'.[2] Cut off from the presence of God in Babylon, the exiled people search for signs of his reality. In memory of their past tradition and acknowledgment of their sin, they experience a new encounter with the God of their forefathers. Memory as a recalling of the past with discernment approaches the act of repentance. Redemptive history continues in Israel's obedient response. Although separated in time and space from the sphere of God's revelation in the past, through memory the gulf is spanned, and the exiled people share again in redemptive history.

(5) The Psalter offers the largest occurrence of the verb *zkr*. While it appears in various types of psalms, the overwhelming majority of cases occur in the individual complaint psalms (42.5; 63.7; 77.4, 7; 119.52, 55; 143.5). Somewhat closely allied is the communal complaint (137.1, 6) and the individual psalm of thanksgiving (Jonah 2.8 [7]).

It is important to recognize that the setting for the verb is the complaint psalm. The fact that the psalmist can remember a situation different from his present plight evokes his bitter complaint and fervent plea for aid. The parallel expressions used with *zkr* offer an invaluable aid in determining the range of meaning. Psalm 42 pictures an Israelite cut off from access to the temple (v. 7), and suffering intensely from his apparent rejection (v. 10). His whole being, day and night, thirsts for the presence of God (vv. 2–3). He is reminded by his enemies of his isolation. Then he remembers the past. Not a sentimental recollection, but a vivid participation. He 'pours out his soul' (v. 5). He remembers

[1] W. Zimmerli, *Erkenntnis Gottes nach dem Buche Ezechiel* (Zürich, 1954), p. 45.
[2] W. Zimmerli, *Ezechiel* (BK, 13), p. 152.

himself as part of the worshipping community in Jerusalem keeping the festival. The comfort is shortlived that he will praise God in such a manner, and in despair again he stretches out toward God in memory. Then, indeed, he experiences the steadfast love (*ḥesedh*) of Yahweh (v. 9). The psalmist continues to fluctuate between the hope of being heard and despair at being forgotten.

Psalm 77 presents a similar situation. An Israelite grieves that God has changed his attitude towards him and that he is now cut off (vv. 8–11). Again he strives to establish contact with God. He 'seeks', he 'stretches out' toward God (v. 3). Then he remembers God and the days of old, and the verbs which he uses are noteworthy. He remembers God and 'moans' (*hmh*); he 'meditates' (*śyḥ*) and his spirit 'faints' (*hith'aṭṭēph*); he 'thinks' (*ḥšb*) on the past; he 'communes' with his heart (in v. 7 read *hgh*; cf. LXX) and searches his spirit. In this passage the verb 'remember' appears as a psychological term closely allied to the verbs 'reflect' and 'meditate'. But, as the psalm increases in intensity, reflection becomes participation and actualization.

Psalm 77 presents a difficult exegetical problem which is closely related to our main concern. The first part of the psalm (vv. 2–11) is an individual complaint psalm which pictures the despair of the psalmist in finding God. It is evident from vv. 2–11 that the attempt of the psalmist to make contact with God by projecting himself back to the 'years of long ago' not only fails but actually intensifies his sense of rejection. His remembering issues only in moaning. Suddenly, with no apparent transition, the form changes to a hymn and the tone turns to hope. His remembering results in an actualization of the redemptive history which he then recites.[1] How is this to be explained? Several notable solutions have been offered to deal with this shift. The interpretation of *zkr* is crucial, since it appears in both sections.

The most frequent explanation is a psychological one. Gunkel saw the psalmist asking himself these questions and then answering 'impossible'.[2] Such an interpretation surely undercuts the deadly seriousness of the complaint and does not really explain the change.

[1] Read the *kĕthîbh* in 12a.
[2] H. Gunkel, *Die Psalmen* (4 Aufl., Göttingen, 1926), *ad loc.*

Somewhat akin is the attempt to find the difference in the object of the memory. In vv. 2–11 the psalmist is occupied in an overly subjective way with his own troubles (*grübeln*), while in 12 ff. his thoughts turn to the wonders of the past. However, this clear distinction in terms of object is not reflected in the text. The object of memory in v. 6 is closely paralleled to that in v. 12: 'days from of old' (*yāmîm miqqedhem*) with 'deeds from of old' (*miqqedhem pil'ekhā*). Moreover, the almost identical expressions occur in Psalm 143 as object of the psalmist's memory, and significantly the mood of despair is not altered there.

Begrich has proposed a priestly '*Heilsorakel*' (salvation oracle) which was spoken by a cultic personage in order to explain the shift in tone.[1] This explanation has much in its favour in Deutero-Isaiah and in certain psalms, but in Psalm 77 there is no evidence whatever which would indicate such an oracle.

The most impressive answer within recent years has been proposed by Weiser.[2] He stresses, in opposition to the psychological exegesis, that an event has taken place which interjects a power which is over and above the inner resources of the psalmist himself. Indeed, he now shares in the redemptive events of Israel's tradition. Weiser feels that this circumstance is only explicable in terms of his participating in a cultic festival in which the great events of the tradition are relived. It is not difficult for Weiser to show that the hymnic form as well as the content of the psalm had its origin in the cult.

Nevertheless, there remain several objections to Weiser's solution which do not seem satisfactorily explained. First, there is no indication that the setting for the act of remembering shifted from the psychological in vv. 2–11 to the cultic in vv. 12 f. Weiser attempts a bridge by resorting to a psychological interpretation of v. 11. He has the psalmist saying: 'It has been my own sickness to feel that Yahweh has changed, while the fault really lies with me.'[3] However, in spite of the introductory formula in v. 11, there is no reason to suggest such a softening of the

---

[1] J. Begrich, 'Das priesterliche Heilsorakel', *ZAW* 52 (1934), pp. 81–92, and a summary in Gunkel-Begrich, *Einleitung in die Psalmen*, pp. 243 ff.

[2] A. Weiser, 'Psalm 77. Ein Beitrag zur Frage nach dem Verhältnis von Kult und Heilsgeschichte', *TLZ* 72 (1947), pp. 136 ff.

[3] Weiser, *ibid.*, p. 135.

text or that a change has yet begun. Verse 11 merely summarizes the intense complaint: God does no longer act.

Secondly, Weiser has not seen the full significance of the verb
zkr. The verb is important, because it occurs in both sections of
the psalm and binds them indissolubly together. It is true that
the hiphil of *zkr* occurs in v. 12 in the sense of confess and bears
its usual cultic overtones. Yet the verbs in 12b and 13 are identical with the first part of the psalm and make it clear that the
formal setting has not changed. The psalmist is still remembering
(qal of *zkr*), 'meditating' (*hgh*), and 'reflecting' (*syh*). Cultic traditions play a role in forming the language used in the intense
spiritual wrestling of the psalmist, but this is quite different from
positing a cultic festival as grounds for the change.

Memory as a psychological process is the same in the two parts
of the psalm. The difference is that in vv. 2–11 the psalmist's
remembering results in bitter frustration, whereas in vv. 12 ff.
he encounters God through his memory. The great acts of the
tradition are not removed in past time, but recharged with
energy they again become a present event. The act of memory
forms a bridge which links the psalmist with the God of the forefathers, not because of a Herculean act of self-projection, but
because the events of the tradition possess a power which continues to meet Israel in her struggle. Israel's redemptive history
continues in her memory as the past events of redeemed time call
forth a new response and are again experienced. Actualization in
memory can occur in a cultic act, but it is significant that the
examples deal precisely with those who are cut off from this
possibility.

Ps. 63 pictures the desperate seeking after God which is such a
common motif of the complaint psalm. One reaches the sanctuary
to discover that 'God's steadfast love is better than life', and
breaks forth in praise. The suggestion of the commentators to
identify the sanctuary with the place of asylum has much in its
favour in the light of the concluding verses. Our concern focuses
on vv. 6 ff. Upon his bed at night the psalmist continues to
experience in his memory the presence of God. He 'remembers'
Yahweh; he 'meditates' (*hgh*) on him; his soul 'clings' (*dbq*) to him.
An experience which was originally cultic in nature is continued,

and actualized through a process which is no longer cultic, but individual and highly subjective.

Finally, Kraus[1] has argued rather convincingly for a cultic background in Psalm 137 which reflects the communal complaint. Israel recalls in bitter sorrow the day of Jerusalem's destruction. Her remembering of Zion is far removed from a casual recalling; rather, the violence of the emotions suggest a genuine participation in the shame of Zion. The psalmist places a curse upon himself if ever he fails to maintain his unity with Jerusalem (v. 6). Remembrance approaches commitment. Again the psalmist is dominated by his feeling of separation from the holy land with its institutions which provide access to God.

Lamentations employs the word in a sense closely allied to the complaint psalms of the Psalter. Kraus argues for a cultic setting of the book as a complaint over the destroyed sanctuary.[2] Weiser rejects this hypothesis, but also defends the cultic background.[3] Whatever one decides in this matter, it is significant to observe that the verb 'remember' is not used in the sense of cultic remembrance within these complaints. Rather, it appears in the genre of the complaint psalm with the same general psychological background as is found in the majority of the psalms of the Psalter. Destroyed Jerusalem is personified as a woman who weeps bitterly, and remembers in her suffering her former state (1.7). Likewise, the subject of the complaint psalm in 3.1–20 reflects and grieves over his sorrow with the familiar vocabulary of this genre. The transition from despair to hope in v. 21 offers a good parallel to Psalm 77.

We shall now summarize briefly the role of zkr in the complaint psalm. The use of memory arises often in terms of separation from God felt by an individual or the community. Israel has been denied the established means of access to God (Pss. 42; 137) and she struggles to find him. The centrality of the temple is never explicitly obviated (cf. 43.3), but in the process something new does occur. In the intense struggle to relate to the tradition, Israel encounters again through the medium of her memory the

---

[1] H.-J. Kraus, *Psalmen* (BK, 15), *ad loc*.
[2] H.-J. Kraus, *Klagelieder* (BK, 20), pp. 8 ff.
[3] A. Weiser, *Klagelieder* (ATD, 16/2), pp. 41 ff.

God of the past. Her attention no longer focuses on specific historical events, but on the divine reality who imprinted her history. The vocabulary used to describe the wrestling process indicates the tremendous internalization which has transpired. To remember is to grasp after, to meditate upon, indeed, to pray to God.

V

STUDY OF THE NOUNS

A. ZIKKĀRÔN

THE noun *zikkārôn* (memorial sign) is derived from the qal stem of *zkr*.[1] It occurs 22 times in its singular form, twice in the plural, and once in an Aramaic cognate. In respect to the distribution there are 14 occurrences in the Pentateuch, one of which appears to be in the JE strata (Ex. 17.14), one from the Deuteronomistic editor (Ex. 13.9), and the remainder from the Priestly source. There is one example in Joshua from the Deuteronomistic editor, and three occurrences in the post-exilic prophets. The remaining examples all belong to the Hagiographa.

The meaning of the term can be classified within two broad categories. First, it carries a passive sense of *memorandum*, a thing worthy itself of remembrance. Secondly, its meaning can be active: a memorial which calls something else to remembrance. Occurrences of the first group, the *memorandum*, appear in a variety of books from an occasional early example (Ex. 17.14) to a clear concentration in the late books. There is a broad range of meaning within this general framework. The word can denote memorable deeds (Esth. 6.1), memorable sayings (Job 13.12), remembrance (Eccles 1.11; 2.16), or simply record (Ezra 6.2). The *zikkārôn* was inscribed in a book (Ex. 17.14). Later the

---

[1] J. Barth, *Die Nominalbildung in den semitischen Sprachen* (2 Aufl., Leipzig, 1894), § 196 b, p. 324. There are two anomalous forms which have caused considerable disagreement among scholars. In Eccles 1.11 and 2.16 the construct is followed by the preposition *lě*. F. Delitzsch, *Commentary on the Song of Songs and Ecclesiastes* (Edinburgh, 1877), p. 225, explained this as an alternate form of the absolute. Cf. the suggested reconstruction by A. Goetze, 'Accent and Vocalism in Hebrew', *JAOS* 59 (1939), pp. 446–7. Most probably this is a construction similar to that appearing in Mishnaic Hebrew. Cf. the parallels given in G. A. Barton, *The Book of Ecclesiastes* (Edinburgh, New York, 1908), *ad loc.*, and R. Gordis, *Koheleth—The Man and His World* (2nd ed. New York, 1951), *ad loc.*

term 'book of memorial(s)' developed (Mal. 3.16; Esth. 6.1). There is no observable pattern represented in the passive usage, nor does the word carry any significant theological meaning.

The second group with an active meaning is strikingly different. The overwhelming majority of cases appear in the Priestly writing. Moreover, there is a clear pattern of usage which bears important theological significance for the writers. Our attention will, therefore, be concentrated on this active usage. We shall begin with the Priestly passages and conclude with several examples of non-Priestly usage.

In nine cases the *zikkārôn* is a cultic object: altar covering (Num. 17.5—EVV: 16.40), booty (Num. 31.54), onyx stones (Ex. 28.12 [*bis*]; 39.7), atonement money (Ex. 30.16), breastpiece (Ex. 28.29), and cereal offering (Num. 5.15, 18).[1] In two cases the *zikkārôn* is a cultic activity, blowing trumpets (Num. 10.10; Lev. 23.24). Once it is a cultic festival, passover (Ex. 12.14). According to the usual Priestly idiom the *zikkārôn* is a 'memorial for the children of Israel before Yahweh'. One has only to recall the role of the cult for the Priestly writer to recognize the full significance of the phrase. God has established a covenantal relationship with Israel which expresses itself in his eternal ordinances (*ḥuqqath 'ôlām*, Num. 10.8). Signs and memorials serve within this dispensation of grace both to guarantee and maintain for each generation this eternal relationship.[2] The cultic acts of Israel continually remind God of this eternal covenantal order. The cultic objects and rites act to guarantee that the covenant is not forgotten.

There are two instances in which there is a slight shift in emphasis. In Num. 17.5 (EVV: 16.40) the covering of the altar is to be 'a *zikkārôn* to the people of Israel so that no one who is not a priest should draw near to burn incense before Yahweh'. The *zikkārôn* serves primarily to remind the people rather than God. Nevertheless, the *zikkārôn* is a sign which guarantees the eternal priesthood of Aaron. Ex. 12.14 declares the passover

---

[1]The word has a negative connotation only in Num. 5.15, 18.
[2]Cf. G. von Rad, *Die Priesterschrift im Hexateuch*, pp. 186 ff.; *Theologie des Alten Testaments*, I, pp. 231 ff., 241 ff. (cf. ET with revisions, pp. 232 ff., 241 ff.); C. A. Keller, *Das Wort Oth* (Basel, 1946), pp. 126 ff.

festival a *zikkārôn*.[1] The particular concern of the P writer is not the reliving of a past historical event so much as the maintaining of a reality which indeed entered history, but is now an eternal ordinance (v. 14). The *zikkārôn* stimulates God's memory and his acts of memory are synonymous with his acts of intervention. The *zikkārôn* also stimulates Israel's memory, which produces participation in the sacred order.

The study of *zikkārôn* greatly increases our understanding of the Priestly concept of memory. We have already seen how the verb *zkr* is used in connection with Yahweh's unfolding of his covenant history. The noun also has its provenance within the covenantal structure. Israel's history is thought of as the working out of the one purpose of God which he established in an eternal order. The concern of the Priestly theology is not to relate present Israel to a past event. There is no tension between past and present because the past mediated an eternal order. Rather, the concern is to maintain the sacred order and relate Israel to it. The memorials as cultic objects serve to insure Israel's relation to God's order by reminding both God and Israel. Yahweh is reminded of his purpose with Israel and his memory is equivalent to his action. Israel is reminded of the eternal order and she again relates herself to it by cultic participation in the events which mediated the order. The Priestly terminology conceives of history as the unfolding of the divine purpose through the interaction of divine and human memory.

There are two examples of *zikkārôn* in the post-exilic prophets which also reflect a cultic usage. In Zech. 6.14 the crown in the temple is a cult object which is closely related to the Priestly theology. Isa. 57.8 used the word in a pejorative sense of idolatrous cult symbol.

Finally, there are two Deuteronomistic passages in which *zikkārôn* appears in its active sense directed to the memory of Israel. In Ex. 13.9 the law of unleavened bread is to be a 'sign on your hand' and a 'memorial between your eyes'. The law is to replace in Israel the cultic marks of the pagan neighbours. The

---

[1]V. 14 belongs with the unit 1–13. Cf. H. Holzinger, *Exodus* (Tübingen, 1900), p. 38, and M. Noth, *Das zweite Buch Moses* (ATD, Göttingen, 1959), p. 73 (ET, p. 94), *contra* Baentsch and Driver.

particular Deuteronomic interpretation of the law as the embodiment of divine revelation explains the nature of the memorial.[1] The memorial does not serve, as in P, to point beyond itself to an established order, nor does it accompany the revelation. Rather, the law of unleavened bread as the expression of the divine will has become the memorial itself. It actively reminds Israel of her responsibility in relation to the Torah. Israel's life is obedient in so far as it is a continual meditation upon the divine instructions (Deut. 6.4 ff.). Because the Torah is a dynamic expression of Israel's relation to Yahweh, each new generation must be continually reminded of Israel's redemption (Deut. 11.19; 30.11 f.; Josh. 1.8). The *zikkārôn* reactivates the original event in Egypt (v. 3). By participating in this event Israel reaffirms her relationship with Yahweh. Therefore, the memorial actively serves to the end that the law of Yahweh be in Israel's mouth (v. 9b).

In Josh. 4.7 the stones are a memorial to God's great act at the Jordan. By looking at them the event is ever a present reality which is passed on to each generation (cf. Ex. 12.26 f.; 13.14). Here the memorial points beyond itself to a specific historical act. The usage differs somewhat from Ex. 13.9, but does closely resemble the Deuteronomic concept of memory which we discovered when investigating the verb.

What can we say regarding the origin of the word and its role in Israel's faith? We have observed that the word was employed with two different meanings. Significantly, the word in its active sense carries cultic connotations with it in almost every instance. Conversely, the passive is usually non-cultic in character. The latter usage is too varied to designate any one area as the context of its origin.

Although the cultic usage is confined chiefly to the Priestly source, we feel that the evidence clearly indicates that the cultic usage has very ancient roots. First of all, the noun occurs apparently as a technical term 'offering of remembrance' (*minḥath zikkārôn*) in the law of the ordeal of the suspected wife (Num. 5.11 ff.).[2] This law goes back to a very primitive stage in Israel's

---

[1]Keller, *op. cit.*, pp. 34 ff.
[2]The precise meaning of this phrase still remains uncertain. Beside the standard commentaries cf. the following important treatments: B. Stade,

development and was obviously not a free creation of the Priestly writer. Secondly, the Deuteronomistic interpretation in Ex. 13.9 presupposes an earlier, cultic usage of *zikkārôn* which is then spiritualized. The law of unleavened bread is to serve Israel in the same way as cultic signs and memorials which one binds on one's hands and between one's eyes.

While we are insisting on the early date of the cultic usage by a priestly circle, it seems most unlikely that the non-cultic meaning can be understood as a later development from the same cultic roots. The word in the passive sense of *memorandum* shows no connection with the cult. A more plausible suggestion is that both usages go back originally to the general psychological meaning of the root *zkr*. Very early the term assumed a specific cultic meaning in priestly circles, while at the same time the word continued to develop in non-priestly circles. However, our study of P's theology has pointed out some of the theological reasons which determined the particular meaning assigned to the word. Within the framework of the covenant God's memory serves in realizing his eternal purpose with Israel. It is significant for the Priestly theology that the verb is not used to relate Israel to this redemptive order. Rather, Israel relates by establishing cultic memorials. Apparently, the Priestly writer found the noun more suitable than the verb for describing this cultic role.

B. ZĒKHER

The noun *zēkher* (name) occurs 23 times in the Old Testament. These occurrences range over a wide historical period. There are two early examples in Exodus (3.15; 17.14), two from Deuteronomy (25.19; 32.26), and a possible example in Hos. 14.8.[1] The largest concentration is in the Psalter (11×) and the later books, although significantly there is no example appearing in the P stratum.

ZAW 15 (1895), pp. 166 ff.; J. Morgenstern, 'Trial by Ordeal among the Semites and in Ancient Israel', *Hebrew Union College Jubilee Volume* (Cincinnati, 1925), pp. 113 ff., especially p. 141; R. Press, *ZAW* 51 (1933), pp. 121 ff

[1] There is some question whether the text in Hos. 14.8 is in order (cf. *BH*). However, there is no compelling textual evidence which would demand emendation. Hos. 12.6 is obviously a gloss.

The word is used as a parallel to *šēm* (name) in five cases, [1] and in four more places this identification is evident from the context.[2] At times *šēm* and *zēkher* are used with no apparent distinction in meaning (Prov. 10.7; Hos. 12.6), but often a basic distinction is still discernible. The *šēm* is the name which has been spoken while *zēkher* describes the act of utterance.[3] The former is the result of an action; the latter the action itself. Yahweh reveals his essence to Moses in his eternal name (*šēmî lěʿôlām*), while the cultic pronunciation of the name throughout the generations is his *zēkher* (Ex. 3.15).

Because the name is the expression of a person's essence in Hebrew thought, the destroying of one's name is synonymous with annihilation (cf. Jer. 11.19; Job 18.17). A similar situation is true of the *zēkher*. If a name cannot be uttered, it is soon forgotten. A large number of passages deal with the destruction of the enemy by means of cutting off all mention of the name.[4]

Then again, there are two passages in the Psalter which indicate a slight broadening of the basic meaning of utterance of the name. In Ps. 6.6 the psalmist complains that 'in death there is no *zikhrekhā*, in Sheol who can give thee praise?' He suffers not because of the inability to *remember* Yahweh in death, as the word is often translated. Rather, the parallelism indicates that the problem arises from the failure of the dead to share in the praise of Yahweh which characterizes Israel's worship (cf. Ps. 88.11; Isa. 38.18).[5] A similar broadening occurs in Ps. 145.7: 'They shall pour forth praise (*zēkher*) of thy abundant goodness.'[6]

[1] Ex. 3.15; Isa. 26.8; Ps. 135.13; Job 18.17; Prov. 10.7.

[2] Hos. 12.6; Pss. 30.5; 97.12; 102.13; *zēkher qodhšô* of Pss. 30.5; 97.12 has its obvious parallel in *šēm qodhšô*, which occurs with great frequency in Leviticus, Ezekiel and the Psalms.

[3] B. Jacob, 'Beiträge zu einer Einleitung in die Psalmen', *ZAW* 17 (1897), p. 70; cf. O. Grether, *Name und Wort Gottes im Alten Testament* (Giessen, 1934), p. 170, where the author contrasts name and word.

[4] Ex. 17.14; Deut. 25.19; 32.26; Isa. 26.14; Pss. 9.7; 34.17; 109.15; 112.6; Eccles 9.5; Esth. 9.28.

[5] There is no need to emend the noun into a participle once the correct meaning of the noun is seen.

[6] Weiser, *Die Psalmen* (ATD), *ad loc.*, translates *zēkher* as '*Gedächtnis*' and sees here a proof for the cultic actualization (*Vergegenwärtigung*) in the cult. This can hardly be read from this verse. The verb *nbʿ* has as its basic meaning 'to speak ecstatically' and expresses always a pouring out of praise or folly, never the actualizing of past events.

In Esth. 9.28 the noun is related to the problem of actualizing the past. The verse reads: '. . . that the days of Purim should not fall into disuse among the Jews nor should their *zikhrām* cease among the descendants.' The sentence would make good sense by translating the noun either by 'commemoration' or 'memory'. However, in the light of our study up to this point, a more consistent meaning would be 'the recounting of them'. The oral tradition must not cease! The past is kept alive primarily by the story. Obviously the meaning is not far removed from that of memory, but it is important to see that memory is only a derived meaning of the noun.

Finally, one of the most important verses is Ps. 111.4: 'a *zēkher* he has made for his great acts.' With few exceptions the noun has been translated by the word 'memory'. Kraus interprets the *zēkher* as relating to the cultic institution by which the memory of the great acts of the tradition was kept alive.[1] In our opinion, this is not a precise exegesis of the text. We agree that the term is obviously cultic, but what is established is not the memory, rather the proclamation of the great deeds. As early as 1897 B. Jacob suggested this translation (*Kundgebung*).[2] The closest parallel in thought to this passage is found in Ps. 78.5:'He established a testimony (*'ēdhûth*) in Israel . . . that the next generation might know.' Clearly there is a close relationship between cultic proclamation and memory. The proclamation consists in the redemptive tradition which is remembered. Yet again, it is important to see that *zēkher* is only secondarily related to memory. The emphasis lies with the act of proclaiming. We conclude that in this passage as well as throughout the rest of the Old Testament, *zēkher* has retained a meaning consistent with its basic meaning of describing the act of utterance.

What can we say regarding the origin of the word and its role in Israel's faith? We have seen that the word occurs chiefly in the hymns of the Psalter, closely allied with *šēm* (name). We have also noted the very ancient roots of the word in the early strata of the

[1]Kraus, *Psalmen*, II, p. 768.
[2]B. Jacob, *op. cit.*, p. 70. It is true that the absolute form followed by the verb is unusual in the Old Testament. In all other instances *zēkher* is followed by a suffix or the construct state. This construction is most likely to be explained by the needs of the acrostic form of the psalm.

Pentateuch. It seems evident that the word arose within the worship of Israel. The name of the deity must be cultically pronounced.[1] This conclusion has been further sustained by our study of the hiphil form of the verb which means 'to name the name'. The noun *zēkher* is the name which is being named. The word has only a secondary connection with the qal form of the verb 'remember'. We conclude, therefore, that the word is not used primarily as a means of renewing the redemptive traditions of Israel, and that it should be carefully distinguished from *zikkārôn*.

[1] Cf. O. Grether, *op. cit.*, p. 176.

VI

MEMORY AND CULT

The evidence which has appeared from our study of *zkr* must now be brought to bear on the problem of Israel's cult. Our analysis revealed that the phrase 'God remembers' had its provenance (*Sitz im Leben*) within the cultic life, in the complaint and in the hymn. The complaint brought a plea for God to remember, the hymn praise that he had remembered. A common meaning was shared by both these forms. God's remembering issued in his intervention on Israel's behalf based on his previous commitment to Israel. The role of the cultic memorials (*zikkārôn*) was to bring Israel constantly to God's attention, which would result in his gracious aid.

It is important to recognize that this cultic understanding of God's memory is not an actualization of the past. The problem of making a past reality contemporary is not involved in God's memory. God is in no sense confined to the past within the barriers of time and space. He is always present. The question at issue in the cult is whether God will continue to act in Israel's behalf as he did in the past or withdraw his aid because of her disobedience.

Turning to the phrase 'Israel remembers', our analysis revealed that the verb had no roots in one specific area of Israel's life, but arose out of the general sphere of human psychological behaviour. In this general sense it was employed widely throughout all phases of Israel's life. To remember was to call to mind a past event or situation, with the purpose of evoking some action. The most significant result of our analysis was to discover that in certain instances the term lost its general psychological sense to take on a highly theological meaning. To remember was to actualize the past, to bridge the gap of time and to form a solidarity with the fathers. Israel's remembrance became a technical term to express the process by which later Israel made relevant

74

the great redemptive acts which she recited in her tradition. The question of how to overcome the separation in time and space from the great events of the past became the paramount issue.

Although the same verb *zkr* is used to express both God's and Israel's remembering, the comparison makes evident that a totally different process is involved.[1] Only in terms of Israel's memory can we correctly speak of an actualization of a past event. Only in relation to Israel's memory is the problem to contemporize past tradition.

Recent Old Testament scholarship has been almost unanimous in pointing out that the chief function of the cult was to actualize the tradition.[2] Israel celebrated in her seasonal festivals the great redemptive acts of the past both to renew the tradition and to participate in its power. Noth summarizes this consensus when he writes: 'There is in the Old Testament the legitimate phenomenon of an actualization of past events which occurs in the cultic, liturgical context.'[3] Israel's tradition bears unmistakable signs of being transmitted in a cultic form.

However, the fact that Israel's cult served chiefly to actualize her tradition raises a serious problem in regard to memory. We have just emphasized that the verb 'to remember', when used in respect to Israel, carried the intense theological connotation of

---

[1]This distinction is blurred by those who seek a general cultic context for memory without sufficient differentiation. Cf. H. Gross, 'Zur Wurzel ZKR', *BZ* 4 (1960), pp. 227–37; M. Thurian, *The Eucharistic Memorial,* I (ET, London and Richmond, Virginia, 1960); and to some extent H. Haag, 'Gedächtnis', *Lexikon für Theologie und Kirche,* 4 (2 Aufl., Freiburg, 1960), pp. 570–72.

[2]In spite of precursors S. Mowinckel's work was basic, *Psalmenstudien,* II (Kristinia, 1922), pp. 16 ff. Cf. also *Le Décalogue* (Paris, 1927), pp. 114 ff.; *Religion und Kultus* (Göttingen, 1953). The following have also made a contribution: M. Noth, *Das System der zwölf Stämme Israels* (Stuttgart, 1930), pp. 61 ff.; A. Weiser, *Glaube und Geschichte im Alten Testament* (Stuttgart, 1931), pp. 35 ff.; A. Alt, 'Die Ursprünge des israelitischen Rechts' (1934) in *Kleine Schriften zur Geschichte des Volkes Israel,* I (München, 1953), pp. 320 ff.; G. von Rad, *Das formgeschichtliche Problem des Hexateuch* (Stuttgart, 1938), pp. 28 ff. (also in *GSAT*); A. Alt, 'Die Wallfahrt von Sichem nach Bethel' (1938) in *Kleine Schriften,* I, pp. 79 ff.; M. Noth, 'Die Vergegenwärtigung des Alten Testaments in der Verkündigung', *EvTh* 12 (1952/53), pp. 6 ff.; G. E. Wright, *God Who Acts* (London, Chicago, 1952); H.-J. Kraus, *Gottesdienst in Israel* (München, 1954), pp. 122 ff.

[3]Noth, 'Die Vergegenwärtigung des Alten Testament', *EvTh* 12, p. 14.

actualization. How, then, are we to explain the fact that the verb when it comes to mean actualization is not intimately connected with the cult? How can actualization take place both in the cult and in memory without their being some genuine relationship evidenced in the vocabulary?

Assuming that our previous analysis of the verb has been correct, there are several possible explanations:

(1) One could argue that Israel's cult never had the function of actualization of tradition which has been assigned to it. However, in the light of the overwhelming evidence to the contrary,[1] this explanation seems excluded.

(2) It would be possible for the verb *zkr* to be employed somewhat late in Israel's history merely to describe a process which had been functioning without interruption within the cult of Israel from its earliest history. However, there is no evidence to support such an hypothesis. Rather, the context within which the verb appears points to a break with the past in which a new element has entered. The word has been reinterpreted and given its new meaning precisely to express a new approach, not merely to describe the continuation of a traditional form.

(3) One could conceive of two different means of actualization which were quite independent of each other, one through the cult and one through memory. However, we saw that *zkr* is used in a theological sense by those circles deeply involved in the cultic life. Memory as a term for the actualization of tradition did not develop in a context which was removed from Israel's cultic institutions. The evidence does not confirm a parallel development but an interrelation.

(4) Finally, it is possible that the original function of the cult as the traditional means of actualizing the tradition entered a period of crisis. Out of this situation there emerged various attempts to relate Israel to her past in terms of memory. The role of actualization underwent a process of transformation. This is an hypothesis which must now be critically examined.

Our study of Israel's memory (ch. IV) indicated the emergence of a new theological meaning in respect to memory which was concentrated in the preaching of the Deuteronomist, in Deutero-

[1]Cf. p. 75, n. 2.

Isaiah, Ezekiel, and the complaint psalms. Is there any evidence that these four witnesses were concerned with a reinterpretation of Israel's cult as a means of actualizing Israel's tradition?

We shall begin with the Deuteronomist. It is not our concern to offer a detailed exposition of the book, but to bring to bear on our immediate problem the results of recent scholarship.[1] The Deuteronomist had as one of his central problems the reinterpretation of the traditions of Israel to a later generation which had not itself participated in the redemption from Egypt and the Sinai covenant, indeed, as we now know, to a generation separated by centuries from these events. Von Rad writes: 'We have in Deuteronomy the most comprehensive example of a theological re-statement of old tradition in which later Israel contemporized the message of Yahweh.'[2]

In spite of the tremendous variety which was inherited from the tradition, the Deuteronomist managed to fashion it into a unity with the central perspective being Yahweh's absolute claim on the whole people of Israel. In terms of the cult this involved a radical reinterpretation. This is not to imply that we have in Deuteronomy an anti-cultic polemic. Von Rad has convincingly demonstrated that even the framework of Deuteronomy reflects a liturgical pattern, and that the writer stands in the traditions of the old tribal league at Shechem.[3] Yet the preaching of the Deuteronomist breathes a different atmosphere from the cult-orientated tradition. His message has lost the sense of immediacy. The paranetic style directed to evoke a response reflects his concern in finding a basis upon which Israel can again be related to the past.

Along what lines has the reinterpretation of the cult taken

---

[1] The writer is chiefly indebted to the several works of G. von Rad: *Das Gottesvolk im Deuteronomium* (Stuttgart, 1929), pp. 28 ff.; *Studies in Deuteronomy* (ET, London, 1953); *Theologie des Alten Testaments*, I, pp. 218 ff. (cf. ET with revisions, pp. 219 ff.). The following have also been consulted with profit: A. C. Welch, *The Code of Deuteronomy* (London, 1924); A. R. Hulst, *Het Karakter van der Kultus in Deuteronomium* (Wageningen, 1938); F. Dumerluth, 'Zur deuteronomischen Kulttheologie', *ZAW* 70 (1958), pp. 59 ff.

[2] This translation differs slightly from D. Stalker's, *Studies in Deuteronomy*, p. 71.

[3] G. von Rad, *Das formgeschichtliche Problem des Hexateuch*, in *GSAT*, pp. 33 ff.

place? The total claim of Yahweh on his people results in the severance of all connection with those areas of nature which offer opportunity for syncretistic infiltration. The cult is legitimate only 'at the place where Yahweh reveals his name'. The emphasis of the liturgy shifts from concern with ritual minutiae to centre in a joyous expression of thankfulness for Yahweh's benefits which are attributed solely to his election love. The criterion for obedience to the law is established in terms of social responsibility to the weak and disinherited. In a real sense, the sacred traditions of the past have been secularized to accommodate them to a new age (cf., e.g., 14.22 ff.).

The Deuteronomist, however, is faced with an obvious dilemma. If he divorces the tradition from its old cultic forms, how does later Israel participate in her past? Has he fallen into the inescapable trap of being forced to reinterpret the cult to a new generation, but by his very interpretation severed all possible means of a return to the past? The Deuteronomist offers his answer in a theology of memory. The task of later Israel is not to try to return to the events of the past. The Deuteronomist has a clear sense of history and he recognized the challenge of the present moment. Yahweh's redemptive dealing with Israel is not confined to the past, but continues. Israel now stands in an analogous position with the Exodus generation and is called upon to respond obediently to his command. Yet later Israel cannot understand the immediate claims of God upon her except in terms of her tradition. The commandments of the law can only be properly interpreted as events in a redemptive history. To lose the historical perspective with the past is to fall into a sterile nominalism. Israel's memory reveals the continuity in the one purpose of God in history. When the son asks the meaning of the commandments, he is recited the historical tradition of Israel's redemption, and admonished to present obedience (6.20 ff.). Israel's memory reminds her that she is not cut off from the past, but the redemptive action of God continues.

There is a second function of memory in the theology of Deuteronomy. Israel is commanded to be obedient to the commandments *in order to* remember the redemptive history. Our exegesis has demonstrated that memory in this case assumes the meaning of actualization. By keeping the Sabbath holy, later Israel remembers or participates in the redemptive history of her past. The Deuteronomist relativized the cultic tradition in conceiving of it along with non-cultic material simply as a commandment (*miṣwāh*) on which obedience could be tested (5.15; 15.15; 16.12; 24.18, 22). The result is a thorough internalization of the tradition. We feel, therefore, justified in concluding that the concept of memory served a significant role in Deuteronomy's theology in meeting the crisis brought about by a reinterpretation of the cult.

The crisis in the religious life of Israel caused by the exile is reflected in both Deutero-Isaiah and Ezekiel. The temple lay in ruins. God's people were separated from the holy land. This did not mean that the cult suddenly ceased in the exile. Von Waldow[1] has demonstrated in a most convincing manner how deeply rooted Deutero-Isaiah's message was in Israel's cultic life. Nevertheless, his message shows a profound reinterpretation of Israel's tradition. Deutero-Isaiah reminds Israel that she has not been forgotten (44.21). Her sins have been forgiven (40.1 ff.) and she now stands upon the threshold of her redemption which parallels the Exodus from Egypt (51.9 ff.). In the light of this situation Israel's memory has a twofold function. First, memory of the past links Israel with the one great purpose of God in history which encompasses both past and future (44.21; 46.9 f.). Even the exile is bracketed within the divine will. Secondly, Israel need not turn to the past for meaning. God is bringing into existence a new age in which Israel can participate (43.18 f.; 65.17).

The message of Ezekiel concerns itself with Israel's failure to understand the nature of her sin (16.22, 43). However, the day will come when Israel will recognize her true condition. Then she will be overwhelmed with the memory of her sin and loathe her deeds. Israel's redemption takes place in the form of a remembering which issues in the knowledge of God. Her memory turns her both to a repentance for past evil and to a stretching out for God. Even in the exile she experiences anew the same divine reality to which her tradition witnessed.

[1]Hans-Eberhard von Waldow, *Anlass und Hintergrund der Verkündigung des Deuterojesaja* (Dissertation, Bonn , 1953), pp. 63 ff.

We turn finally to the complaint psalms. What evidence is there that Israel's memory assumed a role in relation to some crisis which threatened the traditional function of the cult? The nature of the crisis is different from that found in the prophets because no single historical period is reflected in these psalms. The complaint extended from the beginning to the end of Israel's life. Nevertheless, a crisis is apparent. The psalmist is afflicted by a great variety of trouble. He suffers from bodily sickness, rejection, and exile. All these have in common the effect of separating him from the community of faith and from the God of the covenant. Memory became a key word in a tremendous process of internalization of the tradition. It became the means by which Israel found a new avenue to faith when the older cultic paths had become inaccessible. This was in no sense a conscious reaction against Israel's cult or part of a reform movement. A return to the older forms often remained the highest aspiration (cf. Pss. 42–43). Nevertheless, even when the vocabulary of memory became a part of Israel's worship, the increased intensification associated with the word was carried over into the liturgy (cf. Ps. 105.1 ff.).

In conclusion, we feel that the evidence confirms our theory regarding the relation of memory to Israel's cult as a means of actualizing the past. In times of crisis, when the role of the cult was threatened, Israel's memory assumed a new significance in renewing her tradition.

VII

MEMORY AND HISTORY

ALTHOUGH we have frequently used the term actualization (= *Vergegenwärtigung*) with regard to the tradition, we have not as yet entered into a detailed exposition of what is meant. This omission is due, by and large, to a general uncertainty as to its meaning which reflects itself in a wide divergence of scholarly opinion. On the basis of our study we now feel in a position to turn to this question.

We shall begin by discussing two rival theories of actualization in respect to the Old Testament which serve to raise the central issues at stake. The first theory, represented for example by S. Mowinckel,[1] interprets the concept of actualization not as a category indigenous to Israel, but one which arose out of the mythopoeic thought of the Ancient Near East. Of fundamental importance is the relation of cult to myth. The cult has as its function the renewing of the structure of the world by re-enacting the sacred drama of the myth. In this dramatic recapitulation the content of the myth is renewed, and the participants of the cultic rite experience its elemental power. Mowinckel feels that the content of the drama can be either mythical or historical. Within this framework this distinction is insignificant.[2]

This explanation has contributed a lasting service to Old Testament research by making clear the mythical roots lying at the base of the process of actualization. Nevertheless, this theory has a fundamental weakness which has become increasingly evident.[3] Mowinckel has not done justice to the radical alterations

---

[1]*Psalmenstudien*, II, pp. 21 ff.   [2]*Ibid.*, pp. 25, 45.

[3]There have been many who have criticized Mowinckel's position. W. Eichrodt's consistent argument with theories of mythical pattern still remains trenchant, *Theologie des Alten Testaments*, I (6 Aufl., Stuttgart, 1959), pp. 53 ff. [ET, pp. 98 ff.], etc.; also M. Noth, 'Gott, König, Volk im Alten Testament', *GSAT* (München, 1957), pp. 188 ff. On the general subject of Israel's conflict with natural religion cf. the excellent book of G. E. Wright, *The Old Testament against its Environment* (London, Chicago, 1950).

in Israel's cult which set her apart from the general Near-Eastern pattern. The fact that the myth was replaced by historical events is not of secondary importance, but effected a fundamental change in perspective. For Israel the structure of reality was historical in character and not mythical. These historical events could not be repeated; they were forever fixed in an historical sequence. It is highly questionable whether the cult of Ancient Israel ever had the character of a drama which was re-enacted. The process of historization destroyed this element in the cult along with the myth.[1] Rather, the cult actualized within Israel her solidarity with the forefathers, with those who had actually participated in the Exodus. Old Testament actualization of tradition cannot be identified with a mythical concept.

The second explanation stands at the opposite end of the spectrum and is a reaction against the mythical theory.[2] It understands the role of actualization to be the recital in the cult of the great historical acts of the past which established Israel's existence. These acts share the quality of genuine historical events and are, therefore, non-repeatable, once-for-all in character. Actualization occurs when the worshipper experiences an identification with the original events. This happens when he is transported back to the original historical events. He bridges the gap of historical time and participates in the original history.[3]

In our opinion, this hypothesis is basically correct in attempting to guard the once-for-all historical character of biblical events against the timeless quality of the myth. We would also agree that there is a participation in the original events. The disagreement turns about the question of how this participation occurs. In what sense is it a return to the past? Are the original events stationary? We feel that those who emphasize the historical

---

[1] Cf. von Rad's discussion of the rise of the historical sense within Israel, *Theologie des Alten Testaments,* II (München, 1960), pp. 112 ff.

[2] A representative of this view is M. Noth, 'Die Vergegenwärtigung des Alten Testaments in der Verkündigung', *EvTh* 12 (1952/3), pp. 6 ff.

[3] Kraus, *Gottesdienst in Israel,* p. 127: 'Actualization takes place in Israel not in the manner that the original occasion of the encounter of God with Israel is brought near to the assembled congregation, but rather the congregation is placed within the original situation. The once-for-all character of the *heilsgeschichtliche* events is not dissolved into a kerygma . . . The revelation of God in history is once-for-all.'

element in the process of actualization have tended to ignore the dynamic quality of an historical event. It enters the world of time and space at a given moment, yet causes a continued reverberation beyond its original entry. The biblical events can never become static, lifeless beads which can be strung on a chronological chain. In direct analogy to the 'history-creating' Word of God, the redemptive events of Israel's history do not come to rest, but continue to meet and are contemporary with each new generation.[1] We shall return to this point shortly. We conclude that Old Testament actualization cannot be correctly identified with a return to a former historical event.

To summarize: we are suggesting that neither the mythical nor the historical analysis of the process of actualization are adequate to describe the biblical category. This appears to be a concept which shares features of both yet exhibits a unique character of its own. We shall now attempt to penetrate into this category.

The Old Testament witnesses to a series of historical events by which God brought the people of Israel into existence. These events were placed in a chronological order within the tradition, and never recurred in Israel's history. There was one Exodus from Egypt, one period of wilderness wanderings, one conquest of the land. These events were determinative because they constituted Israel's redemption. In other words, they became the vehicle for a quality of existence, redemptive time and space.

These redemptive events of the Old Testament shared a genuine chronology. They appeared in history at a given moment, which entry can be dated. There is a once-for-all character to these events in the sense that they never repeated themselves in the same fashion. Yet this does not exhaust the biblical concept. These determinative events are by no means static; they function merely as a beginning. Our study of memory has indicated that each successive generation encountered anew these same determinative events. Redemptive history continues. What does this mean? It means more than that later generations wrestled with the meaning of the redemptive events, although this is certainly true. It means more than that the influence of a past event

[1]Cf. von Rad's discussion, 'Typologische Auslegung des Alten Testaments', *EvTh* 12 (1952/3), pp. 25 ff.

continued to be felt in successive generations, which obvious fact no one could possibly deny. Rather, there was an immediate encounter, an actual participation in the great acts of redemption. The Old Testament maintained the dynamic, continuing character of past events without sacrificing their historical character as did the myth.

We saw that the Deuteronomist conceived of later Israel as standing in an analogous position with the Israel of the Exodus. God was working her redemption and Israel was challenged to participate. In the memory of the tradition later Israel continued to share in the redemptive events. This is to say, each new generation was challenged to enter God's redemptive time, to participate itself in the Exodus. The dynamic quality of the Exodus event is seen in the events becoming a vehicle for a reality which then continued throughout Israel's history. The chronological position of the Exodus in Israel's history remained fixed (1250 BC?), but its quality as redemptive event—not just meaning—continued to reverberate in the life of the people. We wish to emphasize that the redemptive content of the Exodus was never divorced from chronological history as such.[1] It was not a timeless idea or a non-historical ground-of-being. Rather, a quality of time entered at the Exodus and this content continued to transform the chronological time of each new generation into redemptive time. Redemptive history continued in the sense that each generation of Israel, living in a concrete situation within history, was challenged by God to obedient response through the medium of her tradition. Not a mere subjective reflection, but in the biblical category, a real event occurred as the moment of redemptive time from the past initiated a genuine encounter in the present.

[1] In his most recent book, *Biblical Words for Time* (London, 1962), pp. 20 ff., James Barr has clearly established his point that the Greek terms *kairos* and *chronos* show a variety of usages in the New Testament and cannot therefore be correlated with two different concepts of time. His book is exceedingly valuable for its negative conclusions. However, it is doubtful whether the proposed method of procedure can make a positive contribution, since it tends to remain almost entirely on the level of descriptive semantics with little cognizance of the depth dimension which form-critical analysis has opened up in the study of words. Cf. the author's review of Barr's *Semantics of Biblical Language*, JBL 80 (1961), pp. 374-7.

Actualization is the process by which a past event is contemporized for a generation removed in time and space from the original event. When later Israel responded to the continuing imperative of her tradition through her memory, that moment in historical time likewise became an Exodus experience. Not in the sense that later Israel again crossed the Red Sea. This was an irreversible, once-for-all event. Rather, Israel entered the same redemptive reality of the Exodus generation. Later Israel, removed in time and space from the original event, yet still in time and space, found in her tradition a means of transforming her history into redemptive history. Because the quality of time was the same, the barrier of chronological separation was overcome.

This explanation raises several fundamental questions. If Israel's redemptive history continues in the successive encounters with the challenge of her tradition, how do these remembered events relate to the original event? First of all, it is essential to formulate the question correctly. We do not have in the Old Testament 'an original event'. What we have are various witnesses to an event. Some of the witnesses are closer in chronological time to the original historical happening than other witnesses. Still, these are all witnesses which point beyond themselves. We are not in a position to ask how the interpreted event relates to the 'objective event'. Rather we are forced to ask: How do the successive interpretations of an event relate to the primary witness of that event? One cannot 'get behind' the witness. There are no other avenues to this event except through the witness.

Of course, this point of view will not pass unchallenged. In the history of biblical interpretation there have been several major attacks upon it.

(1) The most effective and persistent has been posed by the scientific historians who stand in the tradition of the great German positivistic historians of the nineteenth century.[1] Their position is familiar: The methods of historical criticism, especially the science of archaeology, provide a legitimate avenue to the same events recounted in the Bible. The Old Testament account is only one among many of a given event which must be tested on

---

[1] Cf. the position of W. F. Albright, *From the Stone Age to Christianity* (2nd ed., New York, 1957), pp. 25 ff., 82 ff.; *JBL* 77 (1958), pp. 244–8.

the basis of objective evidence. A moment's perusal of Pritchard's *Ancient Near Eastern Texts relating to the Old Testament* will dispel any doubts as to the many areas of secular history which overlap with the biblical. The goal of research is to recover the uninterpreted fact as it happened. Objective event can be separated from subjective interpretation.

Two criticisms can be made to this approach. The first arises from the side of the historian, especially in the works of men such as B. Croce[1] and R. G. Collingwood.[2] They have pointed out effectively that the analogy of natural science, when applied to the study of history, has severe limitations. History cannot be described as a sequence of events causally linked, but history has an 'inner side' which is the process of thought. The interpretation is not something added to the event, but constitutes the real event. The 'brute fact' theory is a distortion of the essence of history which is the expression of human thought.

There is a second objection from the side of the theologian. While it is true that the external side of the Old Testament witness often has a parallel in extra-biblical sources, the heart of the Old Testament message—how Yahweh redeemed a people—finds its witness only in the Bible. The message of the Bible speaks of the history of a divine redemption which Israel accepted in faith or rejected in unbelief. There is no direct line from a common, outward framework to the heart of this biblical testimony. The faith response, the interpretation, was not something added to the real event, but constituted the event itself. We maintain, therefore, that it is a fundamental error in interpretation to conceive of redemptive history as a series of scientifically verifiable, historical data to which a religious interpretation has been added.[3]

This is not to imply for a moment that the biblical exegete has no need for historical research. It must be employed with the utmost rigour. The point at issue is whether historical research has as its function to illumine the *interpreted* event, or to attempt to play the so-called 'objective' event against its interpretation.

[1] B. Croce, *History as the Story of Liberty* (London, 1941).

[2] R. G. Collingwood, *The Idea of History* (Oxford, 1946). Quotations are made from the reprint (New York, 1957).

[3] This is basically the issue between von Rad and F. Hesse (*Theologie des A.T.*, II, pp. 8 ff.).

We resist the effort to identify historical research with the philosophical presuppositions of historicism.

(2) Another attempt to get behind the witness has been put forth by the school of modern historiography. We shall concentrate our attention on R. G. Collingwood, whose brilliant book presents the most incisive analysis of recent years. We have already noted Collingwood's criticism of historicism in which he rejects a method drawn from the natural sciences as being valid for historical study. The task of the historian is to understand historical events by re-enacting the process of thought in his own mind. The distinction between subjective and objective is dissolved precisely because the historian must take his stand within, not outside of, the history which he is trying to understand. 'For even when the events which the historian studies are events that happened in the distant past, the condition of their being historically known is that they should vibrate in the historian's mind, that is to say, that the evidence for them should be here and now before him and intelligible to him.'[1]

The historian exercises his critical function by cross-examining his sources and securing information which he can use in his own reconstruction. The historian is his own authority and his thought is autonomous. He possesses a criterion to which his so-called authorities must conform and by reference to which they are criticized. This criterion is his *a priori* historical imagination, by which is meant the sense of a coherent and continuous picture of the past.[2]

A full-scale criticism of Collingwood's concept of history, which would include among other things a detailed examination of his category of *a priori* imagination, lies beyond the scope of our concern and competence. However, we would like to examine the theory in the area in which it impinges upon biblical criticism.

Collingwood properly rejects the attempt to isolate the uninterpreted event. The past can only be recovered by re-enacting the process of thought. On the basis of critical historical imagination the historian can penetrate the uncritical testimony and create his own interpretation of what really happened. But is this

[1]Collingwood, *op. cit.*, p. 202.
[2]*Ibid.*, pp. 236 ff.

not the opposite extreme of historicism which attempts to separate the event from the interpretation? Now the interpretation is divorced from the event. Because the historian shares general human nature, a common mind with the past, he can re-create the real event, which lies only in fractured form in his witness.

While there are some areas within the Old Testament witness to which one might successfully apply Collingwood's method, we feel that the approach would only distort the centre of the Old Testament's witness. The events testified to in the Bible cannot be reconstructed on the basis of an *a priori* category, whether general human nature, or universal experience of the past. Theologically speaking, one cannot measure the radically new with the canons of the old. Again, we maintain that there are no avenues to the history of which the Bible speaks except through Scripture's own testimony to these events.[1]

We return to our original question: How do the remembered events relate to the primary witness? We have concluded from our study that the act of remembrance is not a simple inner reflection, but involves an action, an encounter with historical events. Each successive generation in Israel witnessed in faith to a reality which it encountered when remembering the tradition. The biblical events have the dynamic characteristic of refusing to be relegated to the past. The quality of this reality did not remain static, but emerged with new form and content because it identified itself with the changing historical situations of later Israel. The people of God heard his call to obedience not in the abstract, but through specific historical moments. Redemptive

[1]The most recent attempt in New Testament research to get behind the witness is forcefully presented by J. M. Robinson, *A New Quest of the Historical Jesus* (London, Chicago, 1959). Robinson suggests that the new historiography provides another avenue to the historical Jesus which can be detached from the *kerygma*. Both avenues have in common an existential encounter with the historical Jesus. An adequate criticism of Robinson's position would involve a discussion of the hermeneutical principle underlying the exegetical method of R. Bultmann which is presupposed throughout the book. This lies beyond the scope of our present task. That the question can be approached from a wholly different point of view is seen in the following essays: D. Bonhoeffer, 'Vergegenwärtigung neutestamentlicher Texte', *Gesammelte Schriften*, III (München, 1960), pp. 303–24; P. Meyer, 'The Problem of the Messianic Self-Consciousness of Jesus', *NT* 4 (1960), pp. 122–38.

history is not merely a reflection of Israel's piety—a *Glaubens-geschichte*. Rather, each generation reinterpreted the same determinative events of the tradition in terms of its new encounter. This gives the biblical witness its peculiar character. It consists of layer upon layer of Israel's reinterpretation of the same period of her history, because each successive generation rewrites the past in terms of her own experience with the God who meets his people through the tradition.

In the light of our study of memory we suggest that these successive layers cannot be seen as subjective accretion covering the 'real event'. The remembered event is equally a valid witness to Israel's encounter with God as the first witness. Israel testified to the continuing nature of her redemptive history by the events of the past in the light of her ongoing experience with the covenant God.

Our word study was significant in pointing out that the same verb is used to describe God's redemptive action toward Israel as well as Israel's response in faith to this action. This would indicate that, for the Old Testament, redemptive history is conceived of as resulting from God's action and Israel's response. These elements cannot be separated, nor can they be analysed into objective and subjective components. They form a unity. Because of the nature of Israel's response which we have outlined, an understanding of the redemptive history depends on hearing the witness of all the different layers which reflect Israel's response to the divine initiative. Only in this way can one appreciate the fullness of the redemption which revealed itself in Israel's history.[1]

[1]This study was almost completed when the dissertation of C. L. Kessler came to my attention: *The Memory Motif in the God-Man Relationship of the Old Testament* (Northwestern University, Evanston, 1956). Kessler offers many good insights, but because his approach differs so sharply from mine, little help was afforded. The recently announced book of P. A. H. de Boer, *Gedenken und Gedächtnis in der Welt des Alten Testaments* (Stuttgart, 1962), has not been seen.

INDEX OF AUTHORS

Albright, W. F., 13 n. 3, 85 n. 1
Alt, A., 47 n. 2, 48 n. 1, 75 n. 2
Anderson, B. W., 48 n. 3

Baentsch, B., 54 n. 1, 68 n. 1
Barr, J., 7, 18, 19, 20, 21, 22, 23, 27, 28, 30, 84 n. 1
Barth, C., 22 n. 1
Barth, J., 12 n. 3, 66 n. 1
Barton, G. A., 66 n. 1
Bauer, H., and Leander, P., 12 n. 3
Baumgärtel, F., 37 n. 3
Baumgartner, W., 35 n. 1, 37
Begrich, J., 11, 12, 14, 15, 35 n. 1, 36 n. 1, 41 n. 1, 48, 62
Bentzen, A., 38, 58
Berggrün, N., 11 n. 1
Beyerlin, W., 57
Blank, S. H., 37 n. 2
Blau, J., 11 n. 1, 12
Boecker, H. J., 15 n. 3, 32, 41 n. 2, 48 n. 3, 56
Boer, P. A. H. de, 89 n. 1
Bonhoeffer, D., 88 n. 1
Brockelmann, C., 31 n. 3
Brown, Driver, Briggs, 10
Bultmann, R., 88 n. 1

Childs, B. S., 84 n. 1
Collingwood, R. G., 86, 87
Cooke, G. A., 13 n. 3, 24 n. 2 and 4
Cornford, F. M., 27 n. 1
Cowley, A., 24 n. 5
Croce, B., 86
Cushman, R., 27 n. 1

Dahl, N. A., 26 n. 1

Delitzsch, F., 66 n. 1
Driver, G. R., 24 n. 4
Driver, S. R., 12, 68 n. 1
Dumerluth, F., 77 n. 1

Eichrodt, W., 81 n. 3
Elliger, K., 43 n. 1 and 3

Galling, K., 13 n. 3
Gemser, B., 48 n. 3
Gesenius, W., 9 f. n. 3
Gesenius-Buhl, 11
Goetze, A., 66 n. 1
Gordis, R., 66 n. 1
Greenberg, M., 14 n. 2
Grether, O., 12, 14 n. 2, 71 n. 3, 73 n. 1
Grønbech, V. P., 28
Gross, H., 57 n. 2, 75 n. 1
Gunkel, H., 35, 36 n. 1, 41 n. 3, 61

Haag, H., 75 n. 1
Harrelson, W., 48 n. 3
Hesse, F., 36 n. 3, 86 n. 3
Holzinger, H., 68 n. 1
Hulst, A. R., 77 n. 1

Jacob, B., 10 n. 3, 12, 71 n. 3, 72
Jean, C. F., and Hoftijzer, J., 24 n. 3
Jenni, E., 47 n. 3, 52 n. 2, 53
Jensen, A. E., 28 n. 6

Keller, C. A., 67 n. 2, 69 n. 1
Kessler, C. L., 89 n. 1
Kessler, W., 48 n. 1
Kittel, G., 34
Kittel, R., 39 n. 1
Knudsen, J. A., 23 n. 2

Koehler, L., 9 n. 2, 11, 13
Kraus, H.-J., 36, 64, 72, 75 n. 2,
  82 n. 3

Leeuw, G., van der, 28 n. 6
Lévy-Bruhl, L., 28
Lidzbarski, M., 13 n. 3

Meyer, P., 88 n. 1
Morgenstern, J., 70 n. 2
Mowinckel, S., 42, 48 n. 1, 75 n. 2,
  81
Muilenburg, J., 48 n. 3, 58

North, C. R., 58 n. 1
Noth, M., 48 n. 3, 56 n. 1, 68 n. 1,
  75, 81, n. 3, 82 n. 2

Pedersen, J., 11, 17, 18, 19, 20, 21,
  22, 23, 28, 29, 30
Peritz, I., 10 n. 3
Pfeiffer, E., 48 n. 3
Press, R., 70 n. 2
Pritchard, J. B., 86

Rabast, K., 47 n. 2
Rad, G., von, 7, 34 n. 1, 37 n. 2,
  43 n. 1, 48 n. 1 and 2, 51 n. 1,
  53 n. 4, 67 n. 2, 75 n. 2, 77,
  82 n. 1, 83 n. 1, 86 n. 3
Radin, P., 28 n. 6
Rendtorff, R., 40 n. 1
Reventlow, H. Graf, 11, 15, 16,
  32, 33

Robert, A., 59 n. 1
Robinson, E., 10 n. 3
Robinson, J. M., 88 n. 1
Ross, G. R. T., 27 n. 2
Rowley, H. H., 58 n. 1

Schottroff, W., 7
Schmidt, H., 36 n. 1
Schwally, F., 10 n. 3
Seidel, M., 10 n. 3
Stade, B., 69 n. 2
Stalker, D., 77 n. 2
Stamm, J. J., 11, 13, 47 n. 1
Sykes, H. M., 16 n. 2

Thurian, M., 75 n. 1
Torczyner, H., 24 n. 1

Waldow, H. E. von, 79
Weiser, A., 56 n. 1, 62, 63, 64 n. 3,
  71 n. 6, 75 n. 2
Welch, A. C., 77 n. 1
Wellhausen, J., 54
Wendel, A., 36 n. 2
Westermann, C., 35 n. 1, 37 n. 3,
  38
Wildberger, H., 56 n. 1
Winton Thomas, D., 48 n. 3
Wolff, H. W., 32 n. 1, 39 n. 2
  and 3
Wright, G. E., 7, 48 n. 3, 54 n. 1,
  75 n. 2, 81 n. 3

Zimmerli, W., 43 n. 2, 44 n. 1,
  48 n. 1, 59, 60

INDEX OF REFERENCES

Genesis

1.1–2.3	47
8.1	43
9.15, 16	43
18.5	22
19.29	43
30.22	41
40.14	10, 15, 32, 45
40.23	45
41.9	14
42.9	45, 47
50.20	30

Exodus

2.24	43
3.15	70, 71
6.5, 8	43
9.21	19, 23
12.14	67, 68
12.26 f.	69
13.3–10	54, 55
13.3	10, 33, 46, 55
13.5	55
13.9	66, 68, 69, 70
13.14	69
17.14	66, 70, 71
20.8 ff.	53
20.8	45, 47, 55
20.24	12, 13
23.9	53
23.13	12, 13
28.12, 29	67
30.16	67
32.13	36
39.7	67

Leviticus

19.34	53
23.24	67
26.42, 45	43, 44

Numbers

5.11 ff.	69–70
5.15	14, 67
5.18	67
10.8, 10	67
11.5	29, 45
15.39, 40	45, 47
17.5	67
31.54	67

Deuteronomy

4.23	46
5.12 ff.	53, 54
5.12	55
5.14	52
5.15	46, 52, 53, 54, 79
6.4 ff.	69
6.20 ff.	78
7.18	10, 46, 51
8.1 ff.	50–51
8.2	46
8.11	18
8.18	10, 46, 54
8.19	18, 54
9.6 ff.	51
9.7	46, 49, 51
9.27	36
10.19	53
11.19	69
14.22 ff.	78
15.12 ff.	54
15.15	46, 47, 52, 79

Deuteronomy—contd.

16.3	46, 53
16.9 ff.	54
16.12	46, 52, 55, 79
23.8	53
24.9	46, 47, 51
24.17 ff.	54
24.18	46, 47, 52, 79
24.19 ff.	54
24.22	46, 52, 79
25.17	46, 51
25.19	70, 71
30.11	69
32.1 ff.	48
32.6–7	49
32.7	46, 55
32.26	70, 71

Joshua

1.8	68
1.13	33, 46, 54
1.16	54
4.7	69
7.5	22
23.7	12, 14
24.1 ff.	57

Judges

8.34	46, 49
9.2	45
16.28	18, 36

I Samuel

1.11	36
1.19	18, 41
4.18	15
25.31	24, 32, 45, 47

II Samuel	
8.16	15
13.33	19
14.11	45
18.18	12, 13
19.20	19, 23, 32, 45, 47
20.24	15

I Kings	
4.3	15
5.9	22
17.18	14

II Kings	
9.25	45, 47
20.3	36

I Chronicles	
16.12	46, 49
16.15	31, 41, 42, 45
18.15	15

II Chronicles	
6.42	36
24.22	46

Ezra	
6.2	66

Nehemiah	
1.8	35
4.8	46
5.19	32, 38
6.14	10, 38
9.1 ff., 16 ff.	49
9.17	46
13.14, 22, 29, 31	38

Esther	
2.1	10, 46, 47
4.13	29

Esther—contd.	
6.1	66, 67
9.28	16, 71, 72

Job	
4.7	42
7.2, 7, 7–10	38
10.9	38
11.16	10, 46
13.12	66
14.13	38
18.17	71
21.6	46
28.18	16
36.24	46
40.32	46

Psalms	
6.6	71
8.5	33, 35
9.7	71
20.4	36
20.8	12, 14
22.28	46
25.6	35, 36
25.7	32, 35
30.5	71
34.17	71
38.1	14
42.1 ff.	60–61, 64, 80
42.5	46, 49, 60
42.7	46
43.3	64
45.18	12, 13
63.1 ff.	63, 64
63.7	18, 42, 60
69.13	18
70.1	14
71.16	14
74.2	33, 35, 36
74.18	35
74.22	33, 36
77.1 ff.	61–3, 64

Psalms—contd.	
77.4	46, 60
77.7	18, 46, 60
77.12	14, 45
77.13	18
78.1 ff.	49
78.5	72
78.35	46
78.39	33
78.42	46
79.8	32, 35
83.5	16
87.4	15
88.6	33
88.11	71
89.48	31, 36, 37, 45
89.51	33, 36, 37
97.12	71
98.3	41
102.5	22
102.13	71
103.7, 14	42
103.18	46
105.1 ff.	42, 80
105.5	46, 49
105.8	41, 42
105.42	35, 41
106.1 ff.	42, 49
106.4	18, 33, 35
106.7	46
106.45	41
109.15	71
109.16	46, 49
111.4	72
111.5	41, 42
112.6	71
115.7	18
115.9–11	42
115.12	18, 41
119.49	35, 36
119.52	46, 49, 60
119.55	16, 46, 49, 60
132.1	32, 36

Psalms—contd.

135.13	71
136.1 ff.	42
136.23	18, 41
137.1 ff.	64
137.1	46, 49, 60
137.7	32, 35
143.5	46, 60
145.7	71

Proverbs

6.32	22
10.7	71
31.7	46, 50

Ecclesiastes

1.11	66
2.16	66
5.19	46, 50
9.5	71
9.15	46
11.8	46, 50
12.1	46, 50

Isaiah

1.2	56
6.10	22
10.7	30
12.4	13, 14
17.10	45, 50
19.17	15
23.16	16
26.8	71
26.13	12, 13
26.14	71
38.3	33, 36
38.18	71
40.1 ff.	79
43.18	46, 50, 53, 79
43.25	32, 41
43.26	14
44.6–8	58
44.21	46, 50, 58, 79

Isaiah—contd.

46.8	19, 46, 49, 50
46.9	49, 58, 79
47.7	10, 19, 46, 50, 58
48.1	12, 14
49.1	12
49.14	18
51.9 ff.	79
54.4	46, 50, 58
57.8	68
57.11	19, 33, 46, 49, 50, 58
62.6	15
63.7	14, 49
63.11	31, 45, 46, 58
64.4	46, 58
64.8	32, 35
65.17	16, 50, 59, 79
66.3	14

Jeremiah

2.2	32, 41
3.16	19, 45
4.16	15
11.19	16, 71
14.2–6	39
14.7–9	39, 40
14.10	18, 32, 40
14.11–12	40
14.21	35, 36
15.15	37, 41
15.17, 18	37
17.2	45
18.20	33, 37
18.21	37
20.8	37
20.9	45
23.27	18
23.36	45
31.15–20	40

Jeremiah—contd.

31.20	33
31.34	33, 41
44.21	18, 19, 33
51.50	10, 19, 45, 50

Lamentations

1.7	46, 64
1.9	46
3.1–20	64
3.19	31, 45, 46
3.20	46
5.1	33, 35

Ezekiel

3.20	16
6.9	46, 50, 59
6.10	59
16.22	46, 50, 59, 79
16.43	46, 50, 79
16.60	43
16.61	50, 59
16.62	59
16.63	46, 50, 59
18.22, 24	16
20.43	43, 50, 59
20.44	59
21.28	14, 15
21.29	14
21.37	16
23.19, 27	46, 50, 59
25.10	16
29.16	14
33.13, 16	16
36.23	59
36.31	46, 50, 59

Hosea

2.19	16
6.1–3, 4–6	39
6.11–7.2	39

Hosea—contd.

7.2	32
8.8, 11, 12	39
8.13	32, 35, 39
9.9	32, 39
12.6	70, 71
14.8	70

Amos

1.9	45, 46, 50
6.10	12, 14

Jonah

2.8	46, 49, 60

Micah

1.2	56
2.1 ff.	57
3.1 ff.	57
6.1–5	57
6.3–5	49, 56
6.5	45, 50, 56
6.6 ff., 9 ff.	57

Nahum

2.6	45

Zechariah

6.14	68
10.9	46, 50
13.2	16

Malachi

3.16	67
3.22	46, 50